Clinical Values

Emotions That Guide
Psychoanalytic Treatment

 *Psychoanalysis*
In a New Key
Book Series

Donnel B. Stern, Ph.D., *Series Editor*

Clinical Values

Emotions That Guide
Psychoanalytic Treatment

Sandra Buechler

THE ANALYTIC PRESS

2004   Hillsdale, NJ   London

Published by
The Analytic Press, Inc., Publishers
101 West Street
Hillsdale, NJ 07642

www.analyticpress.com

Designed and typeset by
Christopher Jaworski, Bloomfield, NJ
qualitext@verizon.net

Typeface: Baskerville 11/13

Index by Leonard S. Rosenbaum

Library of Congress Cataloging-in-Publication Data

Buechler, Sandra
Clinical values : emotions that guide psychoanalytic treatment /
    Sandra Buechler
p. cm.
Includes bibliographical references and index

ISBN 0–88163–377–1
1. Psychoanalysis.   2. Emotions.   I. Title

RC506.B836   2004
616.89'17'–dc22
2004041049

Printed in the United States of America
10 9 8 7 6 5 4 3 2 1

*For George, Eric, Zöe,
Michelle, and Nick*

Contents

What seems to me crucial in enabling the analyst to steer a course midway between claims to objectivity on the one hand and invisibility on the other is a love of the analytic inquiry itself and a deep appreciation of the awesome complexity of the human mind.

—Stephen A. Mitchell, *Hope and Dread in Psychoanalysis*

I want to beg you, as much as I can, dear sir, to be patient toward all that is unsolved in your heart and to try to love the *questions themselves* like locked rooms and like books that are written in a very foreign tongue.

—Rainer Maria Rilke, *Letters to a Young Poet*

And sometimes, in the analytic relationship, action must precede thought and word, because the action expresses something unconscious for both patient and analyst. Because it is something unknown and unnamed, it can become known only by being inhabited and lived out in the treatment.

—Stephen A. Mitchell, *Hope and Dread in Psychoanalysis*

To let each impression and each germ of a feeling come to completion wholly in itself, in the dark, in the inexpressible, the unconscious, beyond the reach of one's own intelligence, and await with deep humility and patience the birth-hour of a new clarity: that alone is living the artist's life: in understanding as in creating.

—Rainer Maria Rilke, *Letters to a Young Poet*

A genuine hopefulness about the analytic process is not possible in any real way at the beginning but is something attained only through struggle; it takes great courage. Current psychoanalytic literature is becoming increasingly sophisticated regarding just how difficult and dangerous it is for a patient to use an interpretation in a personally meaningful, truly hopeful fashion.

—Stephen A. Mitchell, *Hope and Dread in Psychoanalysis*

. . . for at bottom, and just in the deepest and most important things, we are unutterably alone, and for one person to be able to advise or even help another, a lot must happen, a lot must go well, a whole constellation of things must come right in order once to succeed.

—Rainer Maria Rilke, *Letters to a Young Poet*

Preface and Acknowledgments

I have taken some linguistic liberties, hopefully far fewer than Lewis Carroll's Humpty Dumpty, who brazenly declared that when he uses a word "it means just what I choose it to mean—neither more nor less." For the sake of convenience I have called the treatment participants "patient," and "analyst," or sometimes "clinician," or "therapist." Generally, I am referring to a treatment process informed by the psychoanalytic literature, most especially, work emerging from interpersonally oriented analysts. I have avoided getting bogged down in making fine distinctions, or in reviewing this voluminous literature. Rather, for each topic I address, I have tried to convey what my own clinical work has taught me.

Out of concern for the privacy of my patients and supervisees I have gone to great lengths to protect their confidentiality. While nothing is made up, some clinical illustrations are fusions of my work with two people, while others are carefully disguised.

Analysts hope to inspire a spirit of inquiry. This book addresses the question of how we accomplish this and is, itself, a product of nurtured curiosity. To name all who have encouraged me would be a daunting autobiographical task.

I will mention only a few people who made this book possible. Shirley Johnson, with untiring good humor, prepared the manuscript.

Many colleagues at the William Alanson White Institute, most especially Jim Garofallou, Richard Gartner, and Marylou Lionells, generously read early drafts. My peer supervision group (Mark Blechner, Richard Gartner, John O'Leary, Allison Rosen, Bob Watson) has provided a professional "family" for more than 20 years. My own family and friends, most especially George, Eric, Zöe, Michelle, and Nick, and my steadfast friend Judith Tick encouraged me to persist. Numerous patients, candidates, teachers, and supervisors, and my own analysts, helped shape my thinking. The William Alanson White Institute has been a superb intellectual home base for me, for many years. But three people, Mark Blechner, Paul Stepansky, Donnel Stern really enabled me to write this book. Many ideas were developed in correspondence with them. Their support gave me courage. Their kindness made me feel less alone. Their honest feedback bolstered my own integrity. Their genuine intellectual curiosity was contagious. I brought my own strong sense of purpose, but they ratified it. They contributed vastly more than their titles (Paul Stepansky, publisher; Donnel Stern, editor; Mark Blechner, cherished friend) suggest. I am profoundly grateful.

Introduction
Manifesting Clinical Ideals

The vast literature on psychoanalytic treatments informs more than it inspires. It fails to integrate life experience into its body. Too often it is content with explanation rather than wisdom. It cultivates intellect at the expense of feeling and spirit.

This tendency in our literature has several unfortunate consequences:

1. Life experience is often felt to be more of a liability than an asset. Those who come to the field with this asset are made to feel inadequate rather than advantaged.

2. Clinicians are not encouraged to integrate what they have learned from literature, from art, and from political activity into their work.

3. Our clinical theories aren't sufficiently evocative to be convincing about the potential meaningfulness of the treatment experience. Although intellectually engaging, our theories don't teach us how to make treatment compelling and alive, for both participants. We learn about projective identification and mirror transferences, but we don't hear enough about evoking hope, nurturing a sense of purpose, or eliciting curiosity.

4. Our meta-psychological literature often uses a dull, desiccated language. It isn't enlivened by our grandmothers' stories or Tolstoy's

rich characterizations. When we talk theory, we often lose touch with our own love for life.

Our theories aren't very useful when we are under fire from a patient. In this postmodern era, we can no longer claim to know truth, but only to have a point of view. Thus what we have to offer can seem too provisional to fight passionately for. How can the sacrifices and rigors of treatment remain worthwhile over a lifetime to us, and how can we engender that value in our patients?

Stanley Fish[1] once remarked that the death of objectivity relieves him of the obligation to be right and demands only that he must be interesting. We have all benefited from the sobering postmodern realization that we don't have the last word on how to live a mentally healthy life. We know that we are each affected by our cultural and personal blinders. Our vision is limited by our own defenses, biases, stereotypes, reflexive assumptions, training, and so on. We can't claim any form of objectivity. The most we can hope to assert is that we know our own distortions well and are able to reveal them. Yet abandoned by all absolutes, can we fight for anything passionately?

Treatment is, I believe, inherently a life-and-death struggle. It takes enormous energy and commitment from both participants. I don't think we can muster, sustain, and inspire this over a career if all we believe we have to offer is one among many possible perspectives. Theories making such modest claims appeal to the mind more than the heart or soul. They don't engender enough hope, or joy, to sustain a real fight for life.

This creates a dilemma. It is clearly valuable that we have emerged from the false certainties of earlier eras. We no longer believe we know what material to privilege. No oedipal, transferential, or defensive content is automatically to be prioritized. Figure and ground are not predetermined by a theory that claims to know the truth about psychic functioning. But how do we passionately fight for a health we can't even define? How do we convince others to invest in a process unmoored by central, abiding tenets?

People fight for what they believe in. This assumes something is right enough to be worth the effort. How can we be driven enough for this battle, yet remain open to today's uncertainties? Can the enlightened perspectivist inspire?

---

[1]Quoted in the *New York Times,* January 28, 1994.

Many years ago I treated John, a young outpatient, shortly after he was released from a brief hospitalization. He presented a history of profound childhood neglect in an affectless, matter-of-fact tone. His speech and his movements had a rigid quality. Even my inexperienced eye could see his extreme loneliness. Rituals had more or less taken over his life. There was a proper way to wash, dress, sleep, eat. He spent much of his time and effort making sure he adhered to the rules.

Without the benefit of much theory or training, I attempted to get to know this young man. I thought of him as having been starved for attention and concern. Not knowing what to do for him, I vaguely tried to supply some of what I felt had been missing.

In an attempt to respond empathically, I found myself speaking with more than my usual affectivity. I answered much of what he said by adding an affective component. I guessed at what I imagined he must have felt while going through his mechanized routines.

I did not really think about this patient diagnostically, and I wasn't concerned about what could happen if I broke through his schizoid and obsessional defenses. My only aim was to supply the missing affect in his speech and, more generally, in his life.

Like many instances of sincere, highly motivated clinicians treating severely disturbed patients early in their careers, I believe I did this man some good. About two years into the work, he began prefacing descriptions of his activities with something like "You would say I felt anxious (or angry, fearful, happy, etc.)." I was much encouraged by this change, feeling it to be progress. We worked together for about four years, during which the patient seemed to loosen up. He got into college and I felt there was some chance he could function well enough to create a viable social and academic life. I heard from him many years later, and he seemed to be doing well.

What happened? Did I do anything more than just improve this patient's vocabulary for affective experience? Would I work any differently with him now?

I'd like to believe what would change most is how I would think about John and his treatment, but not so much what I would actually do. I hope I would still experiment as I did then, creating a language and a way to work together.

But now certain concepts that I have developed over the years would accompany me as I worked with this patient. I believe these ideas would help me bear the process. With them I would feel less profoundly lonely. In a 1998 paper, I tried to distinguish the clinician's inevitable aloneness from painful loneliness. We can't help being alone sometimes, the only one who knows how hard we are trying and what we are attempting to do. But we can be less lonely if our minds are furnished with familiar concepts and well-established inner supervisory objects. These intimately known ideas and identifications can ground the analyst who is venturing to experiment with technique. These concepts help me feel I am still *me*, doing the work my way, even though I am in some respects working differently from how I usually do.

First among these framing ideas for me is the concept of the emotional system. Being a patient requires enough curiosity, hope, joy, and love to sustain the work. It is sometimes necessary to be able to bear surprise. Often anger is an essential motivating force to drive the work forward. I have seen patients fight for their lives, partly in an angry response to obstacles. But the patient's level of shame, guilt, contempt, sadness, depression, and loneliness must be bearable enough for treatment to continue. Too much shame can make the self-exposure of being a patient too painful to go on. Too much anxiety can prohibit risking change. If the patient is too lonely in the treatment hour, she may not find the will to keep working.

I have been deeply influenced by my reading of emotion theory and its conception of the place of emotions in human functioning (Izard, 1971, 1972, 1977; Buechler and Izard, 1980). For me many concepts from this theory have direct clinical application. I make liberal use of ideas from emotion theory in my work. For example, the conception of health that informs my sense of the goal of treatment includes a place for each of the fundamental emotions (Izard, 1977). Human beings respond to life with joy, surprise, sadness, anger, fear, shame, guilt, and other emotions. I believe that we each have a "theory" of healthy emotionality that plays an important role in our clinical work, but frequently the analyst has never articulated this theory and is not aware of its sources or impact. I try to spell out my own personal use of emotion theory in this book.

With my patient John, for example, basic tenets of emotion theory could provide a shared language about life. This goes beyond being able to talk to him of joy, curiosity, shame, anger, fear, and guilt. It also goes beyond lending me absolute conviction that he was subject to all of the emotions common to human beings, whether or not he could presently be aware of them. Furthermore, it goes beyond assuming that discriminating nuances of differences among his emotional experiences would be vital to the treatment.

Emotion theory provides tenets about being human. It includes the assumption that emotions are fundamentally adaptive. They are, at essence, not experiences to be reduced. Some may be unpleasant, and many may have to be borne, but even with these it is primarily *other emotions* that will help. Curiosity can often delimit anger or fear. Shame and guilt modulate the expression of other emotions. Love affects all of what we feel, as well as what we do. Emotions are the most powerful modulators of other emotions. They motivate us and are central to our conceptions of ourselves. Part of how I know myself is by knowing how I characteristically bear anger, for example. I believe it is crucial to the development of a person to become active in finding ways to use anger productively, when that is possible.

Had I known emotion theory when I worked with John, I would have brought to the work a strong conviction about the part emotions play in human experience. I still would have had to experiment with how to talk to John about emotions, but I would have understood more about the meaning of being able to attach words to felt experiences. More crucially, I would have brought rich cultural, theoretical, and personal resources to our work. Every lesson I have ever learned about being an emotional human being would be available to me when I was with John. Every experience I have had trying to use anger, fear, shame, and guilt productively would be with me. Emotion theory gives the analyst and patient a language in that it provides a set of assumptions about the role emotions play in life. With John, I instinctively focused on the absence of expressed emotions, but I felt I was groping. With emotion theory I think I would have felt less alone in the work. I also would have brought to it a set of beliefs that could have allowed me to tap into all of my experience of being human as I tried to make contact with John.

I imagine that now my work with this patient would be easier for me. For one thing, my conception of the human challenges we all face would equip me with ideas about what to *listen for* in the patient's language. But I also think that I would feel less alone. Now, while in the presence of this profoundly unemotional, unconnecting man, I could inwardly relate to my own analysts, supervisors, teachers, writers, and others who have contributed to my understanding of the clinical situation. Because of this I might now feel more whole.

Looking back on my work with John, I believe that supplying an emotional vocabulary wasn't just my way of helping him become comfortable with affect. It also expressed my own determination to stay vividly alive in the treatment. Talking about feelings helped *me* bear the schizoid pulls toward lifelessness that I felt in myself, in response to John. Our refusal to coast through the session can be crucial to the encounter. To reach John, I first had to combat the schizoid in me.

The first eight chapters of this book spell out the qualities I now consider crucial to the clinician's "aliveness." Curiosity, hope, kindness, courage, purpose, emotional balance, the ability to bear loss, and integrity are aspects of our equipment for sustaining ourselves. Together they form the part of our inner resources that links all our experience being human with our conduct of treatment.

H. S. Sullivan (1940, 1953, 1954, 1956) is a tremendously important part of the inner resources I bring to clinical work. For as long as I can remember, he has played a major role in guiding me. My understanding of his precepts has led me through many clinical hours. I find myself using his concepts frequently to shape my role in the treatment exchange. Sometimes with a patient, an idea of Sullivan's will tell me about what I might inquire more. At other times, Sullivan provides me with ways to gather clinical observations into coherent patterns. Overall, his ideas help me function with patients by directing my gaze. Part of my objective in this book is to communicate my way of clinically translating some of Sullivan's thoughts into action in a treatment hour.

Sullivan's greatest impact has been on my focus during the hour. Sullivan tells me what is most important to clarify. If I had had Sullivan with me when I treated John, I would have felt less alone as I decided how to handle his rigid washing, eating, and sleeping rituals. Sullivan would have helped me focus on the interpersonal function of the rituals as their meaning, rather than looking for symbolic meanings. If bathing "properly" for two hours in the morning precluded having breakfast with anyone, this limited social exposure might be central to the meaning of the ritual, and not just a secondary and unfortunate by-product.

With Sullivan as a guide I might have asked the patient, early in the work, *when* he bathed, rather than why it had to be so perfect. Asking why may lead the patient to repeat the obsessional rationalizations. When a behavior occurs and how it affects interpersonal life may inform us more about its purpose and meaning.

Guiding us in where to look, Sullivan accompanies us in an otherwise lonely task. The therapist is often profoundly alone deciding on which of myriad possibilities to focus.

John knows he needs to bathe "properly," and he knows he'd rather have breakfast alone. What he doesn't understand is the relationship between these two preferences. Informed by Sullivan, his analyst can focus on a connection that makes the ritual more meaningful.

What do I gain from this? I have a clearer sense of what I am listening *for*. I am trying to help the patient make connections—not between experiences he knows to be related, but between experiences he had not previously connected. The way I often explain this is that people can easily connect "C" with "D," but they frequently need our help connecting "C" with "H."

This approach saves time. Important material is available *now*. Both participants must constantly contribute. An analysis is not a mystery to be solved by an expert sleuth. The patient is not there to be decoded. Each participant has a different contribution—the patient is the only one who knows her experiences, but the analyst brings a sense of where to focus.

Because this way of thinking gives the material shape, both participants can have hope. It is easier for them both to believe in the process. The analyst is much less alone, in that he has a collaborator in the patient as well as his own internal theoretical guide. Had I an understanding of Sullivan when I treated John, I believe it would have been a different experience for us both.

Along with concepts drawn from emotion theory about the balance of emotions and Sullivanian conceptions about how to focus the material, a third major influence for me is Erich Fromm (1941, 1947, 1956, 1964a, b, 1968, 1973). His conceptual heritage has affected me directly through my reading but also indirectly through his impact on my analysts, supervisors, and teachers. Fromm's attitudes about being human have had a powerful impact on me. Fromm imparts spirit. His voice has helped me define what I am striving for in my work. His concept of biophilia, the love of life, for example, contributes to my sense of treatment's goals. Without Fromm's spirit, the passionate purpose that is at the heart of the work would be missing for me.

Fromm would have given my work with John a clearer sense of purpose. Here was a young man killing his own spontaneity with deadening rituals. Fromm helps me have conviction that what I am doing is important. I am not performing an intellectual exercise. I am fighting in favor of life. For John power resided in the rules, not in him. Fromm strengthens my spirit—inoculates me, one might say, against burnout, cynicism, submission to society's pressures. With Fromm as a guide I feel less likely to succumb to the pull to accept passively the status quo (as dictated by society, or any other authority). Just getting through time and escaping life is not good enough, for John, or for me with John. Blindly following orders (e.g., from managed care) would be as stultifying for me as John's rigid rules were for him. Fromm's spirit sustains my active involvement in the work. Nietzsche remarked, "If we have a 'why' we can live with any 'how.'" This is so for the analyst, as well as the patient. The analyst can bear the strain of doing treatment if she has a strong enough sense of its purpose.

In each chapter of this book, I discuss what I consider to be vital ingredients in treatment—for both participants. I name these ingredients with words we all use in our everyday lives, like courage, hope, curiosity, and so on. My goal is to bridge our experience as parents, children, readers, and clinicians. I don't think treatment survives, and thrives, unless these ingredients are manifested. In this book's first chapters, I address each quality separately and describe how I believe the clinician can summon it in herself and her patient.

Briefly, I have come to believe that curiosity, hope, kindness, courage, purpose, emotional balance, the ability to bear loss and integrity are qualities that we (ideally) manifest—not by design, but as a result of the impact of training and clinical experience on our personalities. Training, we hope, brings out our potential for manifesting these qualities. Our best clinical work manifests them vividly enough to reach the patient.

This is now how I believe I had an impact on John, without consciously having planned it. Although I had not yet been trained analytically, I had enough hope, courage, and so on to connect with him, and he brought out my own potential for these qualities. In a way that I think often happens early in a career, John moved me enough to bring out the native passion in me. He was mysterious enough to arouse my curiosity and vulnerable enough to evoke my kindness. Sufficiently clearly for me to see it, he showed me that our work can effect how fully a person lives his life. John's well-being was palpably on the line. This brought out my own courage and sense of purpose. Even though I had not yet had the analytic training that, I believe, can confirm our commitment to treatment, heighten our clarity of purpose, and cultivate our curiosity, John was able to bring out these qualities in me and I, in turn, inspired him to reach for "more life."[2]

But to cultivate these qualities in training, our language must be jargon-free. We become wooden when we use jargon. It is as though we morph into an emotionally cut-off self-state. While aware of our membership in a special professional culture, we lose touch with the rest of our human experience. We forget what it means to hope that our children lead full lives or that our parents find the courage to fight illness. Jargon disconnects us from the wellspring of vital feelings. If we do not stay in touch with these essential inner resources, we will be unable to inspire passionately. I think of curiosity, hope, kindness, courage, purpose, emotional balance, integrity, and the ability to bear loss as essential to forging a treatment that can effect real change in how a life is actually lived.

The last chapter of this text deals with how theory, married to life experience, can sustain the clinician's efforts. My experience tells me that passionate commitment to doing treatment is getting even harder to maintain. We need to manifest our own alive curiosity, hope, kindness, courage, purpose, emotional balance, integrity, and ability to bear loss. We can't kindle these feelings if we have not connected their presence in sessions with their place in our own lives. To animate theory, we need to remember everything we have learned about life and bring our whole selves to work. Only then can we recognize moments that are opportunities. Each treatment hour can be understood as a dialogue about these ideals. Every session challenges the analyst to find her focus, language, and purpose. From those who have profoundly affected us, we each forge a treatment style, which we then modify continuously. I believe that our "style" really emerges from our own struggle to maintain the curiosity, hope, kindness, courage, purpose, emotional balance, ability to bear loss, and integrity that treatment requires.

Patients take us to familiar and unfamiliar places. To cope well with the strain of this encounter, we have to avail ourselves of all our inner resources. Professional mentors, life experiences, cultural examples, and theoretical concepts potentially enrich us and prepare us for this challenge. Exactly what we need to summon depends partly on the

---

[2]To quote from Tony Kushner's play, *Angels in America*.

human dilemma the patient is currently facing and his characterological ways of coping with life. This book is my attempt to show how an analyst can use inner resources to accommodate the shifting therapeutic demands.

Treatment can only be truly effective if it is lived as a microcosm of the fundamental challenges of life. To do this adequately, I must respond to each moment in treatment with my whole being. When I am fully present with a patient, I am listening, but I may also be remembering something from Shakespeare's *King Lear,* or H. S. Sullivan's conception of parataxic distortion, or something I went through in my own life, or something one of my supervisors, or analysts said. In any case, if I am surrounded by many of these memories, I am not alone. I am, often, inspired to go on. I have a sense of direction. Unpredictable phrases spring to mind. I am a reader and a woman. This moment, with this patient, is about meeting the unending challenge of being a curious, hoping, kind, courageous, purposeful, balanced, integrated human being. Anything that informs me about such struggles is relevant. To bear the strain of helping so many people, I had better avail myself of my whole grasp of life. I had better listen to everyone who has ever told me a story, touched me, and taught me.

1   *Evoking Curiosity*

I want to beg you, as much as I can, dear sir, to be patient toward all that is unsolved in your heart and to try to love the *questions themselves* like locked rooms and like books that are written in a very foreign tongue. Do not now seek the answers, which cannot be given you because you would not be able to live them. And the point is to live everything. *Live* the questions now.

   . . .

For if we think of this existence of the individual as a larger or smaller room, it appears evident that most people learn to know only a corner of their room, a place by the window, a strip of floor on which they walk up and down. Thus they have a certain security.

—Rainer Maria Rilke, *Letters to a Young Poet*

These lines were written by Rilke to a young man who asked for the poet's advice as to whether he should become a writer. The young man, Franz Xaver Kappus, is impatient and wants "The Answer,"

Dr. Donnel B. Stern's input was especially central to the development of this chapter.

now! The 10 letters Rilke wrote to help guide the anxious fledgling have been published as the *Letters to a Young Poet.*

Rilke responds to the youth's urgency with wise and gentle advice. In these letters, written from 1902 to 1908, Rilke recommends patience. He advises Kappus to maintain an open mind and not to succumb to easy, ready answers simply to have an illusion of clarity.

Rilke's (1934) humility about being able to help Kappus can serve as a warning to clinicians: "For at bottom, and just in the deepest and most important things, we are unutterably alone, and for one person to be able to advise or even help another, a lot must happen, a lot must go well, a whole constellation of things must come right in order once to succeed" (pp. 23–24).

How does the clinician encourage the patient to "live the questions now"? How do we elicit openness to new experience, willingness to experiment, tolerance of uncertainty and ambiguity? How do we sustain our own open minds and alive curiosity?

Instinctive Curiosity

In this chapter I reflect on what interferes with curiosity and what elicits it, in treatment and elsewhere in life. I believe there is a continuum, from curious open-mindedness to paranoid closed-mindedness. Curiosity and paranoia are opposites, in their response to the unfamiliar (for a discussion of the absence of curiosity see D. B. Stern, 1983). To stimulate the patient's curiosity in treatment, we have to address paranoia's pervasive pull, in ourselves and in the patient.

If we watch an infant eagerly exploring, we may be puzzled by this issue. Isn't curiosity an inborn proclivity? William McDougall (1908, cited in Izard, 1977, p. 197) defines curiosity as an instinct and highlights novelty as its instigator: "The native excitant of the instinct would seem to be any object similar to, yet perceptibly different from, familiar objects habitually noticed." McDougall suggests that lesser degrees of strangeness elicit curiosity, whereas greater degrees activate fear.

Almost a full century separates us from William McDougall, yet I believe this to be a timely insight for us as individuals, and as a society. Are we intrigued by the stranger, or do we become defensively closed off? Our ability to remain open to the strange and unfamiliar (nonfamily) has great political and psychological significance in our post–September 11, 2001, world. Our society as a whole needs to learn how to find enough that is familiar in the strange(r) to evoke more curiosity than fearful defensiveness. But we also need to find enough that is unfamiliar so as to elicit sufficient active curiosity.

Writing of interest and curiosity, Izard (1977) captures its importance to society, as well as to the individual:

> In a very general sense the psychological significance of this emotion is to engage the person in what is possible, in investigation, exploration, and constructive activity. If people lived in a world that was stable and unchanging forever, then perhaps there would be no need for the emotion of interest. But the fact is that we are in an ever-changing world and have the capacity for the emotion of interest, and our interest will not permit the change and flux to go unnoticed. Our interest makes us want to turn things around, upside down, over, and about. This is because we see some possibility in the object or person or condition that is not immediately manifest to the senses [p. 225].

Interest and curiosity motivate a good deal of our active effort, in treatment and the rest of life. Interest guides as well as motivates us through selective *focusing.* Any session presents both participants with myriad possibilities for focusing on some material, noting other material peripherally, and failing to notice some material at all.

Thus, for example, a patient comes to a session feeling hurt. In the previous session, she had waited for me to notice her new haircut and, perhaps, to comment. I had said nothing, not because I thought commenting inappropriate or because (as the patient supposed) I didn't like the haircut and was being polite, but because I didn't notice the haircut at all (I frequently overlook changes of this kind). My lack of interest focused me away from the haircut, which the patient (mis)interpreted.

Curiosity selects focus for both patient and analyst. This would appear to make their roles similar, and yet, I suggest, they differ in their responsibility for exciting curiosity. The analyst is called on to sustain her own curiosity and evoke it sufficiently in the patient to support ongoing treatment.

To further specify the analyst's task, I briefly describe six functions of the analyst's curiosity, and then consider how she can evoke the patient's ongoing curious self-exploration.

Curiosity as a Clinical Resource

The analyst's curiosity provides some protection from burnout. Maintaining our curiosity can help us balance the pain our work often evokes (see chapters 6 and 9). Like long-distance runners, analysts need sustained momentum. Curiosity motivates us to take understanding further.

More specifically, I believe curiosity is essential to

1. Focus selectively, preventing both participants from becoming overwhelmed by the material.
2. Create a context where other important interchanges can occur (D. B. Stern, 2002, p. 519).
3. Promote the integration of self-states in each treatment participant.
4. Notice what has not previously registered.
5. Expand the material or, in Sullivan's terms (1953, 1954, 1956) conduct the detailed inquiry.
6. Reflect on the countertransference.

After brief consideration of these uses of the analyst's curiosity, I address the process of promoting the patient's self-discovery. Successfully launching this journey makes the difference between a stunted treatment and a much richer, ongoing process. The development of the patient's "analytic attitude" (Schafer, 1983) *toward himself* is key to the results of the work (see chapter 9 for a discussion of the analyst's analytic attitude as a model for the patient's functioning).

Focus

Looking back, then, over this review we see that mind is at every stage a theatre of simultaneous possibilities. Consciousness consists in the comparison of these with each other, the selection of some, and the suppression of the rest by the reinforcing and inhibiting agency of attention [James, 1890, p. 288, in Izard, 1977, p. 134].

I can think of no better description of sessions with patients than "a theatre of simultaneous possibilities." Curiosity heightens the spotlight on some issues, relegating others to the background.

A patient rushes into her session late, unsmiling, speaking rapidly. She is worried about her job and the uncertain economy, exasperated by her boyfriend's psychological obtuseness, and overwhelmed by her mother's chronic anxiety. Barely pausing for breath she recounts the latest episodes in these arenas. None of this is new to us. I feel as though what she is saying is both too much and too little: too much to focus on, yet too little room for meaningful reflection.

I begin to think about her ambivalence about her boyfriend. Should she marry him and try to create a shared life? She presents myriad instances of his inattunement, self-involvement, personal failures, unrealistic demands, and physical unattractiveness. Settling down with him would indeed be settling, in her mind.

Yet I also know she faults herself for her own hypercritical tendencies and inability to compromise. I begin to think about "settling" and "compromising." Are they different? What gives each its personal meaning to her, to me, to human beings in general?

Before I began to think about the question I already knew that, like Rilke's young poet, my patient wanted The Answer that would rid her of each of her problems immediately. Once again I felt the clash between the patient's hopes and my own (Mitchell, 1993; Buechler, 1995b, 1999). I knew I couldn't give her what she wanted, and that, if I tried, I would share her overwhelmed state.

Once I began to think about the difference between compromise and settling, the session took a shape, for me. Some stories seemed more relevant than others. Words acquired new meaning. I listened differently, and heard references to this issue in the patient's choice of words. When she spoke I felt less adrift. I was looking *for* something, not just looking. Some might say this was a loss. I had stronger "memory" and "desire," despite Bion's (1977) often quoted injunction that the analyst should have neither.

And yet, I could function, form thoughts, connect to my countertransference. I could hypothesize as to why her boyfriend might sometimes tune her out, using my own countertransference experience as information.

My thoughts had greater coherence, allowing me to associate to them. My patient's human dilemma evoked some personal reflections on my own life. I could also bring my experience as a reader of poetry, fiction, psychoanalytic theory, and emotion theory to the session. I could wonder what my own analyst would say about "settling" and "compromising."

I believe curiosity and focus are really aspects of each other, fundamentally inseparable. Each makes the other possible. They allow us to bring more to the session, shaping thought enough to give it meaning and, at least potentially, make it communicable.

Therapeutic Context

Curiosity, the desire to use words to understand—the desire that psychoanalysts of all orientations are glad to embrace as their own—is an orienting motive. It sets in motion the kind of interaction within which other things, at least equally important, can take place. You need a task around which to organize the relationship with a patient, because you are not a parent and not a friend; even a parent or a friend interacts with children or friends around some kind of mutual interest. Analyst and patient need to have reason to be together. . . .

Our curiosity is not a mere excuse for other kinds of relatedness. It must be authentic. We must really want to get to know the patient and ourselves, consciously and otherwise. And we must believe that learning these things will help. But in coming together to be curious, we also set up a situation in which other events are possible [D. B. Stern, 2002, p. 519].

Curiosity moves us to wonder "why now?" Why does this patient come for help now, not a year ago, not next year? My training, largely Sullivanian, taught me what Levenson (1991) might call an algorithm of treatment. Clarify the "presenting problem" first and then work on setting the frame and getting a careful history. All the while, attend to fluctuations in the patient's level of anxiety, as expressed nonverbally (through gesture, tone, facial expression) as well as verbally.

Of course no treatment proceeds in such a linear, stepwise fashion. The "frame," which, as Levenson suggests (1991) includes the participants' expectations for the work, is negotiated throughout treatment. The "history" is continuously compiled and amended. Regardless of one's model of treatment and regardless of how much one believes the history is "uncovered" or "cocreated" (Spence, 1982; D. B. Stern, 1997), it is clear to me that it is, at least partially, an exercise in curiosity.

When I meet new patients, I usually want to know how he or she heard of me, and why they chose to see me. I am interested in why they seek treatment now, whether something feels different, or worse, or more urgent. I want to know how long each problem has bothered them. I ask about what I call "the situation" they were born into, because I believe each of us enters life in a cultural milieu, period of human history, socioeconomic context, familial configuration, and neighborhood that shape our experience of being human.

As the patient and I explore his or her history, I am forming, testing, and discarding hypotheses. I am also looking for connections, repetitive patterns, and difficulties that take different shapes as one grows older. For example, I come to understand a woman was severely depressed as a young adult. Might the depression actually go back far enough to help us understand her elementary school isolation?

For the moment I am concentrating on the clinician's curiosity, but I will focus on the patient's shortly. The elaboration of the patient's history and reasons for seeking treatment *now* are clearly fueled by curiosity. A patient tells me about a beloved relative's death, which occurred when she was well into her teens. I ask if she went to the funeral. She did not. I ask why. She is silent. She does not recall ever questioning this. Many other unanswered questions suddenly become salient. The clinician's curiosity, early in treatment, helps create a climate that makes the rest of the work viable.

Making the Strange Familiar

Many years ago I took a course on the metaphor, hoping to better myself as a poet. I don't think it furthered this goal, but it has helped me as an analyst. The basic exercise in the course was to use words to "make the strange familiar, and the familiar strange." I find this a useful way to think about clinical work.

I think of the integration of self-states as making the strange familiar. A patient suffered greatly at the hands of a sadistic father. Now in a position of authority, can she see her own inclination to abuse her power?

A young woman does a great deal of traveling for work-related purposes. She feels different at home, serious and responsible, much like the precociously adult teenager her life forced her to become. When away, however, she is free to enjoy romance, spend money, wear attractive clothing, indulge in her favorite foods, but she is also unable to concentrate on work, even if a pressing deadline necessitates it.

Thanks to a burgeoning literature on normal dissociation (Bromberg, 1998) and a post-9/11 surge of interest in responses to trauma (Gensler et al., 2002), there is a great deal of attention to how we help people develop self-cohesion. I can't conceive of doing this work without the impetus of curiosity. How is my traveling patient the same human being at home and away? How can I help her recognize the traveler in herself at home, and meet the responsible worker while she is having an out-of-town fling?

Making the Familiar Strange

Edgar Levenson has used the aphorism that "the last one to know about water is a fish" to indicate that part of our job clinically is to discover the assumptions that are so pervasively embedded in the patient's outlook that they are unnoticed. I think of this as making the familiar strange. Something the patient takes entirely for granted is questioned by the analyst. Of course the patient also isolates and questions the analyst's assumptions.

Noticing the other person's assumptions, crystallizing them, and inquiring about them takes curiosity. A patient presents a situation she is well aware has become unpleasantly frequent. She and her lover had yet another fight about their weekend plans. She knows this will keep happening, because simply giving in is too reminiscent of humiliating childhood capitulations. The patient expects me either to support that she took a stand or suggest she might have given way in the name of harmony. Instead, I wonder why there are so few choices. This enables us to explore the patient's assumptions.

Expanding the Living Room:
The Art of the Detailed Inquiry

I believe that by making the detailed inquiry the heart of the treatment process, Sullivan (1953, 1954, 1956) highlighted the role of curiosity. In a more recent contribution, Levenson (2003) provides a succinct and vivid description of the process:

> When I do therapy, I like to think of myself as a director perusing a script that I must transform into visual images. How is it to

be played? What are the nuances? As Edelson (1993) explicates the clinical process to students, "Ask yourself as you listen to the patient: Can you see what they are doing? Hear what they are saying?" (p. 317) Sullivan's detailed inquiry essentially explores different scenarios [p. 234].

Over many years Levenson (1972, 1982, 1983, 1991, 2003) has developed an interpersonal approach that emphasizes demystification, elaboration, expansion, and enrichment of the material. Most especially in "Whatever Happened to the Cat? Interpersonal Perspectives on the Self," but also in many of his other writings, Levenson emphasizes the need for the analyst to ask, "What is going on around here?" rather than "What does it mean?" (1991, p. 226).

The "cat" in question belonged to a patient as a child, until it was left in the family's summer home, at the end of a vacation. A session from this patient's treatment was reported by Gill and Hoffman (1982, in Levenson, 1991) and discussed by Levenson (1991). A clear contrast emerges between what Gill and Hoffman focus on and what Levenson questions. Gill and Hoffman are interested in the transference meaning of the patient's associations.

The patient's sense of puzzlement at her parents' behavior and her feeling that she was treated unfairly by them seems to parallel her experience of the immediate interaction with the therapist. He, too, she must feel, leaves her to divine by herself the reasons for the deprivations she is called upon to endure [Gill and Hoffman, 1982, p. 16, quoted in Levenson, 1991, p. 226].

In contrast, Levenson (1991) asks,

What really happened to the cat? Was the poor beast left to die in the basement? Unlikely. Was a window left open? Did a neighbor pick it up later? Did it stay in the basement until they returned the next weekend? They seemed to be leaving at the summer's end. Was the poor cat ever seen again? Is she making up the whole story to indict her mother, the abuser of children and pets? Or, is this an example of a common enough, if deplorable phenomenon, people who desert their pets at the end of a summer, leave them to fend for themselves, become feral? [p. 226].

Both approaches rely on the analyst's curiosity but lead to different focuses. Levenson is looking to expand the inquiry into real events. His mind's eye roves over the picture he formulates of what must have happened in the past. Questions spiral, leading to further puzzles.

I think this encourages both participants to wonder. The analyst is not asking himself to explain what it all means. He is seeing what happens if he turns something over, asks another question, follows wherever it leads. In Levenson's (1991) words, "There is a dimension of creative play, of pleasure taken in developing skills, and of curiosity for curiosity's sake which is underestimated by all metapsychological systems that emphasize developmental pathology" (p. 235).

Levenson (1991) has outlined an "algorithmic" approach to treatment (pp. 115–124). This is a series of three essential steps: establishment of the frame, including expectations about the work; noticing gaps in the material (which enriches the data and reveals defensive operations); and playing out the central issues in the transference–countertransference. In this approach, the analyst's curiosity plays a key role.

For example, a patient recounts a recent conversation with his father. Once again, the patient is invited to join his father in financially providing for his younger siblings. Although the patient can currently afford to do this, the future looks extremely uncertain in his field. Of late, he has spoken of his anxiety about his own financial security.

The patient describes how he quickly agreed to help his siblings, so they would have the "peace of mind" of "extra reserves." I notice much that seems to me to be missing in his account. Where were his usual financial concerns for himself? Where was any feeling about his father's focus on the younger siblings' welfare, and not the patient's?

In this example the gaps, or what is sometimes (Levenson, 1991, p. 118) called the "holes in the Swiss cheese," help me identify areas of defensive operation. By engaging them as I do, I take a position that inevitably enacts a transference–countertransference dynamic.

The analyst's curiosity about what is missing from the patient's story, and why it is missing, enables her to make inquiries that, it is hoped, expand what is knowable.

In the *manner* of the detailed inquiry (Sullivan, 1953) the analyst has many opportunities to live out a stance that emphasizes open-mindedness and individual responsibility without undue emphasis on blame. What attitude does the analyst convey about the patient's parents? Is the *analyst* looking for someone to blame for everything? Furthermore, how does the analyst treat the patient while getting information? Is the feel of the interaction that one person is willing to be interested in temporarily entering the world of the other (in contrast to a paranoid rigid insistence on always remaining within one's own world view)? Does the inquiry feel like an inquisition? Does it have the staccato rhythm of a rapid-fire cross-examination? Is the analyst always thoughtful about how he is treating the patient, careful not to use inquiry as an opportunity for a kind of verbal "rape"? Does the analyst avoid sadistically using what he knows of the patient's vulnerabilities? If so, the patient can have the valuable experience of someone who has the tools, the power, to cause him pain, but chooses not to hurt him if it can be avoided. Similarly when Levenson (1972) curiously looks for the kernel of truth in the patient's delusion (e.g., that his soup is being poisoned), he is passing up an opportunity to label the patient crazy and dismiss the patient's thoughts. I would suggest that when Levenson asks how he might be "feeding him a poisoned relationship" (p. 80), part of why this is therapeutic stems from what Levenson *refrained* from doing. He has a potential weapon, and he doesn't use it. He could simply confirm his certainty of the patient's craziness, but he's more interested in the truth. Also Levenson has not patronized the patient or shown undue credulity by agreeing about the soup itself, but he is willing to see where playing with the thought might lead.

The Analyst's Self-Reflection

A review of the countertransference literature will not be attempted here (see, e.g., Mitchell, 1993, 1997; Renik, 1993; Hirsch, 1995; Buechler, 1999; Maroda, 1999, 2002). It seems obvious that curiosity fuels our wonder about the part we have played in the treatment. I believe it is our curiosity, as much as anything else, that can enable us to use the countertransference as *information* (usually about both participants) rather than as *self-condemnation*. The evolution from countertransference as a source of shame, guilt, anxiety, disgust, anger, and contempt to its productive use is a crucial component of analytic professional growth.

Evoking the Patient's Curiosity

Being curious herself is probably crucial to the analyst's ability to evoke the patient's curiosity. But because I believe paranoid anxiety is curiosity's major obstacle, how that anxiety is handled is also relevant.

Evoking the patient's curiosity is a key factor in treatment's outcome because it can motivate the patient to sustain the work, despite its pain, costliness, and so on. Many interpersonalists (e.g., Sullivan, 1954; A. Cooper, 1969; Witenberg, 1973; D. B. Stern, 1989a, 1990) have commented on this. Witenberg (1973), for example, suggests the following: "The analyst moves toward developing a cooperative relationship with the patient by a careful inquiry into his feelings and attitudes. This inquiry serves to stimulate the curiosity of the patient so that he becomes an active participant in his own treatment" (p. 7).

But, to me, it is not enough for the analyst to be curious. To facilitate curiosity, the analyst must contend with the paranoid tendencies in himself and in the patient.

Paranoid Inhibition of Curiosity

While paranoid defensiveness is not the only inhibitor of curiosity, I believe it is a significant factor. Other issues, such as narcissistic deficit, inhibit curiosity in circumscribed areas of life. (In narcissism, for example, curiosity is curtailed when its pursuit might lead to self-esteem injury. A patient doesn't want to explore whether he would enjoy painting because he is too afraid of the possibility of failure.) But paranoia opposes *all* that is unfamiliar, *because* it is unfamiliar. Paranoia closes off exploration, narrows our vision, insists on its certainties, and delimits pursuit of the paradoxical and the ambiguous. I think of paranoia as, at its essence, in opposition to curiosity's tendency to venture into new territory. Paranoid defensiveness relies on our ability to predict, to be certain, to "know the score" in advance. In a paranoid frame of mind, we need to see the new in terms of the old, in already established categories. We fit the new into old frames. In contrast the curious infant, or clinician, or patient pursues a novel idea, connection, or association, not knowing where it will lead, but wanting to find out.

To understand paranoia fully we must look at what it avoids, as well as what it tries to accomplish. Paranoia eradicates doubt. It opposes surprise, delimits willingness to risk. In its certainty it bypasses ambiguity and ambivalence. It seems to offer a bastion against guilt, shame and depression.

Paranoia Versus Curiosity in Treatment

"If a man will begin with certainties, he shall end in doubts, but if he will be content to begin with doubts, he shall end in certainties" (Bacon, in Barford, 2002, p. 225).

Bacon alludes to the fundamental opposition between the soul of curiosity and paranoia. In treatment, as elsewhere, paranoia seeks a certainty that can anchor, whereas curiosity needs to roam. Paranoia needs to know where it is going before it gets there; curiosity wonders what would happen if. . . . Paranoia loves stereotypes because they give the illusion of foreknowledge. It looks for right and wrong, not subjective shades of gray. It wants to discover, not to create the truth.

Subtly paranoid thinking plays a pervasive role in conflicts between the participants in treatment. It may be the therapist who is aiming for freewheeling exploration of the patient's past, present, and future. This is a sensibility in which curiosity reigns and focus dances from one thought to the next. The mind, unencumbered by any preformulated destination, goes wherever it will.

But to the extent that the patient needs paranoid certainty she will be unable to follow curiosity's lead freely. She will be pinioned by an inner necessity. The need to be right will be stronger than the need to explore. In Rilke's language, she will not love her life's questions and live them fully. She will urgently need to arrive at The Answers. And if living in a small corner of her "room" guarantees familiarity with every square inch, she will cling to that corner with all her might.

Living the Questions: The Challenge for the Analyst

The analyst's behavior must demonstrate the fundamental difference between paranoid and nonparanoid theory building (Kovar, 1966). It is not having a theory that is inherently paranoid, but *how that theory is held.* What I call "holding theories lightly" is what I believe distinguishes therapeutic from paranoid thinking.

Some of the difference between paranoid and nonparanoid thinking resides in how we treat exceptions to our theories. Are they celebrated? If not, we, like the paranoid patient, may be more interested in maintaining a state of certainty than in knowing the truth. How much poorer we would be if some intellectual adventurers hadn't been interested in the exceptions, in the experiment that disconfirmed their preferred hypotheses.

In treatment the paranoid pull invites the analyst to participate in theory building. What is *really* going on, beneath the surface? Help me, the patient seems to ask, read my situation more accurately. The analyst may be recruited into this role, out of a genuine desire to be of help, to feel that the patient and she are collaborating on the same side, and to feel useful. For these and other, more personal reasons, it is often easy to get an analyst to speculate on what is really happening at work, in the marriage, in the family. We can explain this to ourselves as helping the patient to "reality-test." Inadvertently, we may be confirming a paranoid slant on life. Our own dread of uncertainty and distrust of surfaces may join the patient's.

Because paranoid explanations sharpen preferred distinctions and don't make room for paradox, ambiguity, or ambivalence, often the analyst will eventually feel cramped in the cocreated Procrustean bed. There is room for agreement but not for observing shades of meaning. This can profoundly challenge the analyst. How far should he go in his effort to remain an ally? How much should he sacrifice of his own, potentially nuanced vision? At what point does this effort become the analyst's failure to maintain his own integrity (see chapter 8)? How can the analyst avoid externalizing all the responsibility for this dilemma onto the patient?

Treatment of paranoia can become a kind of "high noon" confrontation. Patient and analyst each enter the arena, armed with their theory. Who will prevail? Will the analyst "dodge the bullet," or will he be rubbed out, rendered impotent by the patient? Who can use his theory more adroitly? Who is quicker on the draw? It sometimes seems like an occasion for "fancy footwork." It can take grace to maintain the therapeutic alliance and still retain a sense of self.

The analyst must manifest the self-discipline to postpone the pleasures and comforts of certainty. He must, as Rilke suggests, live and love the questions. He must relish the adventure of going wherever his questions lead more than he worships the stable idealized stillness of certainty. He must maintain his integrity without being classified as an enemy by the patient. The challenge for the analyst is to live out loud, in front of the patient, manifesting a palpably curious nonparanoid stance.

Am *I* willing to know and show my own forgetting, ignorance, and uncertainty enough to ask for information I don't have? If I don't remember something already told to me, am I curious enough to ask the patient to repeat it? Listening to a dream, do I scramble to make "sense" of it? Am I willing to unravel therapeutic material, rather than neatly sew it up? Do I use theory reductively, seductively, inductively, or deductively? That is, how does theory affect my focus in the session? Do I reduce the patient to an instance of my favorite theory, or try to seduce the patient into accepting my hypotheses? Does my theory evolve from my experience of the patient, or is my experience of the patient limited by the dictates of my theory? Although we may congratulate ourselves that we no longer force patients' experiences into a preformed oedipal mold, our theories nevertheless can still compromise our peripheral vision. If I'm looking for "splitting" or "narcissistic injury," or "dissociated affect" or even "health," I am more likely to find it. I live out my relationship to theory every session. (For a more extended discussion of the use of theory, see chapter 9.)

I am suggesting that there are three aspects of how we relate to our own theories that are especially important in helping the patient move from a (paranoid) closed to a more (curious) open stance:

1. The analyst provides a contrast to paranoid thinking by embracing uncertainty and ambiguity. By openly loving unanswered questions, by risking looking ignorant, she so clearly differs from paranoid certainty that the contrast is unmistakable. Whether or not it is consciously formulated by the patient, it is surely *felt*.

2. The analyst invites the patient to join her, in the session, in playful exploration. I call this becoming a "catalyst." We encourage experimenting with new ways of being curious. This *actual interpersonal experience* with a new way of functioning often promotes changes both inside and outside the treatment.

3. The analyst poses what I call a "relational challenge." Even the patient who is unwilling to play with open-ended questions still has to

find a way to deal with an analyst who loves them. If this makes the patient uncomfortable, the discomfort itself can become useful to explore.

Facilitating Wonder, Self-Discovery, and Playful Experimentation

An added consideration for nurturing and preserving curiosity, wonder, and openness in clinical work from D. B. Stern's (1990) perspective involves acknowledging more fully our relationship to the unknown. He characterizes this relationship through the image of a psychoanalytic "doppelganger" that rustles in the echoes of everything that an analyst does or says: "curiosity is the never satisfied insistence on knowing the doppelganger, the unknown psychoanalyst who is there in the room, too, and who will always be just beyond acquaintance, forever moving and forever still, occupying the same shadows on the far side of every new understanding" (p. 472) [Zeddies, 2002, p. 430].

If we have the spark of curiosity in ourselves, how do we pass it on? In his paper, Zeddies describes the difficulties of an analyst who has the capacity to wonder but who wants the patient to feel it, too. How can he make that happen without, paradoxically, stifling the patient's initiative by taking over? In Zeddies's words,

At this point in our work, I was attempting to balance two contrasting ways of being her therapist. On the one hand, I felt that I needed to take a leadership role in her sessions in terms of getting her to talk about emotionally significant events in her life and commenting or interpreting what she said. On the other hand, I wanted to promote a more self-driven or self-initiated kind of self-discovery that I figured could result only from Amber working more actively to construct or lead our interactions [pp. 435–436].

Zeddies goes on to describe how his patient, Amber, came to some important new insights. He posits the existence of a "psychoanalytic unconscious" in himself that helped guide his interventions with Amber and that encompasses "distinctively psychoanalytic values" (p. 441).

I am in complete agreement with all this but, from my point of view, it doesn't fully explain Amber's dawning interest in the meaning of her own reactions. Zeddies sees himself as in a power struggle:

> I was also very aware of her tireless refrain whenever I tried to interest her in looking beneath the surface features of her experience. She would laugh dismissively and insist that I was pulling things out of the air that did not have anything to do with the realities in her life. And there it was. Before I had even voiced an idea, I sensed a familiar power struggle brewing between us: whose perspective of the meaningfulness of her world would win the day? [p. 436].

Despite anticipating her dismissing response, Zeddies persists (p. 437) and attempts to get the patient to self-reflect. Amber answers that as far as she is concerned, Zeddies seems to think that everything is meaningful. "You're the meaning man," she gently chided, "always looking for something even when it's not there."

So why did Amber then engage in some very meaningful self-reflection? Did her analyst's curiosity enable her to wonder too? For me a key piece of the story is Amber's position (p. 438) as the youngest and highest functioning of 11 children in a highly dysfunctional family. As might be expected, Amber assumed a caretaker role, which meant that "Amber's own needs and wishes often go unrecognized or neglected, and she has come to expect that other people (within and beyond her family) are not interested in how she feels and what she thinks."

But Zeddies *was* interested, even interested enough to subject himself to her ridicule. I suggest that Amber understood (in some sense) Zeddies's struggle with himself. She knew he wasn't just curious about her with an unfeeling detachment, as though she represented an interesting specimen. Zeddies, unlike her family, was so interested in "how she feels and what she thinks" that he is willing to be chided by her and internally conflicted about how to work with her. Whether or not we see Zeddies as, in his own terms, "batting for average" (engaging in a slow, cumulative process), what I think matters most is that *he kept slugging*. Despite her initial attitude, Zeddies wanted to know Amber, wanted Amber to know Amber, and wanted Amber to *want* to know Amber.

Zeddies provided the three components I see as vital to facilitating curiosity:

1. He *contrasted,* profoundly and sincerely, with her closed-mindedness.
2. He was a *catalyst,* inviting her to join him and experiment with a new curiosity she could then bring to the rest of her life.
3. He provided a relational *challenge.* He made himself hard to dismiss. He made it difficult for Amber to keep her mind locked shut.

Living the session with curiosity *is* an interpretation when it provides a contrast to the patient's style. To attempt to bear this task, we must palpably care more about opening the patient's mind than about making good points. Our own need to be proven right must not pervade our work, or we will foster dead-end power struggles. So often the need to be right leads to others' argumentative, angry withdrawal (O'Leary and Watson, 1995, p. 405). If we are openly more invested in helping the patient than in showing what we know, we will not iatrogenically create this negative interchange. This will significantly contrast with the patient's paranoid need for risk-free, closed-minded certainty.

The analyst manifests his personal relationship to risk (Mitchell, 1997) in every session. We are always (consciously and unconsciously) choosing which risks to take. Some risk is inevitable—but how far should we go in risking alienating the patient for the sake of getting to the "truth" as we know it? What risks aren't worth it? The analyst weighs risks with every interpretation, and the patient (consciously and unconsciously) observes. What does it say about the analyst's motives that he took this risk but passed up the other? How do our values shape the interpersonal risks we are willing to take? For closed-minded paranoia, risk is a key issue. His analyst helps him most, I believe, by *transparently* juggling risks and thus contrasting with paranoid, tight secrecy about motives.

Often, our risk-juggling is a response to the kinds of questions the patient poses. The patient, lacking crucial pieces of equipment for living, comes to therapy with unanswered questions about life. How does a human being bear loss, risk, uncertainty? How can we know when we are loved and how much is it safe to trust? A paradox inherent in treatment is that the analyst is not a sage and yet must indicate a willingness to respond. In the interest of the treatment we must sometimes have the courage to go out on limbs. We must embrace the paradox of knowing and not knowing, of being expert and nonexpert. We do not have the right or the wisdom to dictate how anyone should live, but, unlike paranoia, we must be unafraid of our uncertainties. We must manifest our commitment to life by responding sometimes when it would be safer to be silent. A patient poses a question, such as, should I leave my wife? We must honestly grapple with the question. Our response must reflect respect for the fact that we don't know "the" answer but we are willing to participate actively in finding "an" answer. Forgoing the paranoid tendency to avoid doubt, we must plunge headlong into the question, bringing all of our resources (Szalita, 1976; Wolstein, 1988; Renik, 1993; Buechler, 1997; Issacharoff, 1997; Maroda, 1999, 2002). The patient will take from watching us grapple that we *do* have good intentions and *are trying to help even at the expense of our own comfortable certainty.* We will have taken the risk of exposing what we do and don't know. We will have embraced the paradox that we are experts in something no one can be an expert in. Knowing that even what we choose to focus on, question, and ignore can slant the outcome, we will have borne, in the interest of the work, the grave responsibility of having an uncertain interpersonal impact. Do I ask the unhappily married patient how long he has been married, whether he was once happy, what he was originally attracted to in his wife? Any one of these questions, or their omission will affect the dialogue. Part of the therapeutic task is to struggle openly with the fundamental questions about life, love, relationships, priorities, and values that come up in the treatment and to find a way to describe that struggle to the patient. At other times, I think we have the greatest impact by understanding some aspects of the material without commenting at all. What we don't ask about or, perhaps, even notice tells the patient a great deal about us as human beings. If the patient says he feels guilty, and I don't ask why, I have revealed a lot about my values. To be of help to the paranoid aspect of the patient, I must be comfortable with the subjectivity, limitedness, and lack of clarity of my impact. Together we may understand my impact better in a year; for now I have to bear, with minimal regret, shame, guilt, loneliness, and anxiety and maximal curiosity, hope, integrity, and courage, the paradox of being an "expert" in the interpersonal sphere (Buechler, 1998, 1999, 2000).

In addition to taking risks and talking about them, I believe that to evoke the patient's curiosity we have to serve as catalysts, openly encouraging the patient to experiment with new ways to relate to us. This promotes the chance that the patient will have experiences inside and outside of treatment that are only possible with a mind open to the new. That life experience can change him.

Finally, I believe we often have to find a way to serve as relational challenges. Levenson's focus on what happened to the cat, and Zeddies's perseverance in searching for meaning both disrupt "business as usual" for the patient.

To provide enough contrast, catalyst, and relational challenge to excite the patient's curiosity, we must ourselves love questions and maintain real openness to new ideas, valuing them no matter what cherished beliefs they counter. We must love the adventure of discovery more than we love the security of certainty. We must have a driving, passionate need to know more than just a corner of our own "room" and to ignite a similar burning desire in others.

2　*Inspiring Hope*

In the treatment of nervous cases he is the best physician who is
the most ingenious inspirer of hope.

　　　　　　　　　　　　　—Samuel Coleridge, *Table Talk*

Although it is clear that the participants in treatment need
hope, the nature of that hope is difficult to define. Hope is an elusive
concept. In this chapter, I take an inductive approach to the question
of hope in treatment. That is, I begin with some of my own clinical experiences and try to glean what it means for the analyst and for the patient to maintain hopefulness about the work. Although I suggest
some differences in what it takes to maintain hope in various therapeutic settings (inpatient treatment, outpatient treatment, psychotherapy, psychoanalysis), I believe all patients' and all clinicians'
hopes are more alike than different, as I elaborate here.

Active Hope in the Patient

During my graduate school years, I worked in a state mental hospital.
Those of us who were able to last on staff were called "key swingers," in

reference to the heavy keys we carried that opened the locked wards, where the more violently disturbed patients lived.

I was still in my 20s when I took the job of staff psychologist, responsible to work with one ward of psychiatric inpatients. Looking back I would say I was an unlikely candidate to make it as a "key swinger." Too young, too inexperienced, too intensely emotional to last.

Some memories from that time are still vivid to me. I remember, in particular, one woman in her 30s, who had the misfortune to "fall between the cracks." That is, as a person with multiple mental handicaps, both mildly retarded and emotionally disturbed, she belonged everywhere and nowhere and had been shuffled from one institution to another most of her life. She had no adult experience "on the outside." Her family had long abandoned her, and she had no marketable skills. Although her history mentioned violent behavior, I could only see a placid, moonlike, round-faced, overweight woman with cheerless eyes.

I decided she was going to leave the hospital. Perhaps I couldn't bear the sadness of her downcast, lusterless eyes. I'm sure I couldn't stand the idea she would never know freedom. To be limited in mental scope *and* locked in an institution seemed, to me, simply too much. But what could she do on the "outside," and how could I get her there?

Anyone who has worked in such settings can imagine the bureaucratic obstacle course that followed. She became a willing partner but still couldn't make the arrangements on her own. As the process took the shape of a plan, with a halfway house, outpatient services, and a job in place, she visibly brightened. Her face seemed less the placid mask, her features more mobile. On the day she left, she told me to "go good and do good, because you are good."

Some capacity for hope had survived in this woman. She still could reach for "more life," as the character Prior Walter advises in Tony Kushner's (1992) moving play.

How come? I used to satisfy myself by assuming that some combination of the patient's innate "drive toward health" (Sullivan, 1953) and my own youthful determination were enough to explain it. But now, 30 years later, I wonder whether her hope, like her parting blessing, was a kind of present to me. I wonder whether hope is often a gift to someone (although not necessarily someone currently alive). Understanding the patient's hope as a gift points to hope's inherent interpersonal nature but still doesn't fully explain its source. As a patient nears our 20th year of analytic work, we can both easily see her greater assertion and freedom, but some of her presenting problems still truncate her life. Depression shadows her, as ever. Her anger can still suddenly overtake her. Her knowledge of sexual desire is still secondhand, gleaned more from movies than experience with her husband. Given the enormous investment of time, money, and effort she has already made, what should give her continuing hope?

In this situation I believe the patient's hope is partly a gift to me. She believes in my integrity, that I wouldn't continue to treat her if I didn't think she would derive benefit from it. She believes in the treatment because she believes in me. Her "gift" to me is enduring trust. No matter how long it takes, she seems to say, she will have faith in my motives and my judgment. If I still think she will benefit, she will still have hope for our work together. I would suggest that, regardless of the setting, if the patient can believe in the clinician's good intentions, the patient can retain hopefulness.

I am attempting to understand the emotional aspect of hope, as well as its cognitive aspect as an *expectation*. Much has been written on the subject of the patient's and the analyst's hopes. S. H. Cooper (2000) succinctly summarized how hope has been seen from a variety of theoretical viewpoints:

> Most psychoanalytic theories also hold in common that the patient looks to the analyst for change and help—that the analyst in some ways embodies hope and expectation for change. Freud (1905) referred to the patient's trusting expectation of change from the analyst as one of the analyst's best therapeutic aids. The analyst also embodies hope for the patient in real and defensive ways within Lacanian approaches (Nasio, 1997). In the developmental tilt (Mitchell, 1988) models of Winnicott and Kohut, the analyst represents the revival of hoped-for objects who might catalyze the true self that has been submerged. Indeed, in all psychoanalytic models, our patients see us as representatives of psychic possibility [p. 260].

But "trusting expectation" is not all I am referring to when I write of hope. I am trying to understand the passionate force of hope. How else can we comprehend patients and analysts bearing the (often) agonizingly slow process?

For both participants, maintaining hope has certain prerequisites:

1. *The willing suspension of disbelief.* We counter our own felt experience (right now we are not getting anywhere) with an article of faith (that says nothing about the eventual outcome. We *will* get somewhere).

2. *An acceptance of mystery.* There is no rational way to explain why an insight becomes possible at a particular moment in time. We may be able to outline our thought process but we can't explain why we saw a connection in December that we didn't see in October.

3. *An acceptance of contradiction and paradox.* Pizer (1998) puts the negotiation of paradox at the heart of the therapeutic enterprise. He credits Winnicott with the initial recognition of the role of paradox in therapy, which many others now appreciate. Pizer sees tolerance of paradox as a fundamental developmental or therapeutic achievement. I feel his emphasis on paradox is particularly relevant to a discussion of hope. For example, both participants have to maintain hope despite knowing that the analyst is not a "wise elder" (in Cooper's sense; see S. H. Cooper, 2000, chapter 10). We know, or come to know, that every perspective, including the analyst's, is flawed and subjective, yet we believe in the process.

4. *Hope and faith are impossible to separate.* Hope in treatment requires faith. The patient and the clinician can't have abiding hope without abiding faith. Faith by definition is "belief that does not rest on logical proof or material evidence" (*American Heritage Dictionary,* 1969). That is, faith inherently does not require proof. Faith in the process is largely really faith in the personhood of the clinician, for both participants.

Hope for the Wrong Thing

One of the ways I have tried to understand the patient's hope is to notice when it is absent and then try to sense why. Mitchell (1993) eloquently described a patient who needed him to join her despair about the treatment in order to emerge eventually into hope. The patient needed to experience her analyst's willingness to stay with her, in her dreadful hopelessness.

In his discussion of this clinical vignette Mitchell (1993) quotes T. S. Eliot's poem "East Coker":

I said to my soul, be still, and wait without hope
For hope would be hope for the wrong thing . . .
Wait without thought, for you are not ready for thought:
So the darkness shall be the light, and the stillness the dancing
[p. 228].

For me this poem crystallizes one of the most fundamental functions of the *absence* of hope. Not having hope when it would be hope for the wrong thing preserves the possibility that some day we will be able to hope for the right thing.

So long as we are limited to the rational, afraid of the paradoxical, unable to accept the terms of life, we will hope for the wrong thing. Any hope we may hold is tinged with the vague knowledge that we won't get that "wrong thing" because it is unattainable. We hope to make cumulative sense of things, to see our lives in straight lines, from deficits to fulfillments, from ignorance to wisdom. But each moment is new, and we are always unprepared for it. Our attempts to "know what we are doing," whether as patient or analyst, only impose misleading meaning and offer false security. To quote again from Eliot (1943):

There is, it seems to us,
At best, only a limited value
In the knowledge derived from experience.
The knowledge imposes a pattern, and falsifies.
For the pattern is new in every moment
And every moment is a new . . . and shocking
Valuation of all we have been [p. 26].

Hopelessness is sometimes a profound self-awareness that one hasn't yet grown into realistic hoping, the way a child hasn't yet grown into an older sibling's clothing. It would be foolish to hope before we are ready. We have to wait without hope, until we understand our lives a bit better.

People often hope for predictably wrong things. The paranoid person wants an impossible certainty. He is happy when his analyst is willing to explore why others treat him as they do. He wants tinkering with his "take" on them. He hopes that with a better grasp on what they *really* mean, he will be able to navigate the interpersonal world more successfully. But he is not optimistic, even when his analyst is willing to go

along with his agenda. Without full awareness he senses his is a losing strategy. The best "take" in the world still doesn't ensure the outcome. His hope for the wrong thing is shadowed by undispellable
uncertainty.

The narcissist hopes for an ego-enhancing self-reflection, but he,
too, has halfhearted hope. He "knows," just under consciousness, that
even if he gets what he is asking for, it won't adequately reassure him of
his worth. Like the eating-disordered patient, he is never really filled.

The obsessional's hope for magical control, through choosing just
the right words to get wished-for effects, fails similarly. He, too, can't
put much faith in his own strategy. The same can be said for the schizoid's maneuvers. The attempt to feel safe by controlling distance from
others inevitably fails. Muting effort, emotional intensity, and interpersonal contact still won't make him feel secure, and he knows it.
Hope for the wrong thing is always faint of heart.

Patients are not the only ones who can hope for predictably wrong
things. A fascinating example was provided in a dialogue between
Richard Chefetz and Philip Bromberg (2002). Chefetz presented his
treatment of Nancy, a dissociated patient. Bromberg then commented:

> I began to hear what had clearly started as a "discussion" about
> Nancy's dissociation, subtly develop an enacted subtext—a part
> of Nancy that seemed to be experiencing Rich's effort to give
> her hope about the future *at that moment,* as a way of his not hav-
> ing to listen to her frustration and anger that her life continues
> to be just too damned hard because all he gives her is insight
> into the fact that she has a lot of different parts, but *she's* the one
> that has to live with them, and still suffers from the fact that it
> hasn't changed [p. 45].

As I understand this, the patient felt her analyst's hopefulness was
in the service of his avoiding truly encountering her suffering. In this
case, I would say the analyst was hoping for something predictably unrealistic, that is, that he could get through his work without feeling pain
intensely.

Both treatment participants often waiver in their hopefulness. For
over a decade, I treated a severely physically disabled woman who came
to treatment burned out and depressed. Her life took too much energy;
even getting on and off the elevator in the morning was an ordeal. The
special car service she used was rarely on time, if it showed up at all.

But her sense of defeat wasn't really about the daunting details of her daily routine. It stemmed from the question of whether a "normal" man would ever want her enough to share her "disabled life."

Her secret hope was that if a perfectly normal man loved her she could feel whole again. Her disability had occasioned many shaming experiences in preadolescence, before it was correctly diagnosed. Her clumsy walk was labeled "lazy" by her critical parents, and when she repeatedly fell, it was blamed on her eating too greedily and letting herself get "fat." So it was all her own fault.

It didn't take long for the patient to find me extremely disappointing. As years went by, this feeling only intensified. I could interpret the patient's wishes and transference oedipally. To her I was the oedipal mother who withheld the profoundly desirable man. She believed that if I really wanted her to find him, I could make it happen. Because it hadn't, I must not want it for her. The patient is often as busy interpreting the analyst's hopes as the analyst is busy interpreting the patient's desires.

These days I question whether I can know the right thing for patients to hope for from treatment. But I still believe I can often spot the wrong thing. Most of the time, I think, the patient knows it too, but not in exactly the same terms as I do. In this case the patient's "wrong" hopes were laced with fear that no perfect lover would ever find her beautiful, striking, unique enough. Her hope was an angry hope, filled with accusations. Why was her analyst born with two good legs, and therefore able to get anything she wanted? This patient introduced me to a new lexicon. In her world people like me were called "TABs"—temporarily able bodied. This is how she expressed her spiteful hope that aging would bring me a taste of the suffering she had to endure throughout her life. Aging would even the playing field. *Then* how would I like it?

I will never forget one particular session, early in our work. The patient was quite depressed and angry at me. The session before, her humiliation was heightened by the fact that she *couldn't* walk out on me without *my* help! If she wanted to leave a session she would have to ask me to help her out the door, just at the moment she hated me most for my "withholding." To have to go to me for help when she wanted to defy me was simply too much to bear. The patient spotted a box of tissues and in what I later understood as a creative flash, she brought them closer to her and, one by one, shredded them on the floor. She had found a vehicle for defiance that didn't require my help.

From my point of view the patient's hopes were for the wrong things—no magically perfect lover or properly chastened analyst would cure her *psychic* disability, that is, the profound narcissistic injury she had endured. She knew this on some level, and that muted the hope she could have for the treatment. She knew that even if she got her every wish from me, her psychic wounds would remain. But she wasn't yet ready to hope better. She couldn't yet hope for something attainable.

This treatment ended abruptly when the patient suddenly died, in her 30s, probably from a complication of her disability. Her progress away from faint, unrealizable hope toward true hopefulness and psychic wholeness, was cut short. You might think I was left feeling as impotent as the patient had (early on) wished me to. But that wasn't so, for she had progressed enough to take care of that before she died. In our last sessions, she made sure I understood my impact on her, by quoting me extensively. When a patient offers me this kind of linguistic mirroring, I feel it is a move toward intimacy, and also a subtle gift of gratitude. She could want me to feel effective, potent, and potency was a treasure to her. Now we both, I felt, could have realistic hopes for her in new relationships. She had come a long way, from bitterness couched as hopes to real, openhearted hopefulness. When she died, I had deeply conflicting reactions. Oh no, not now! Not when we were finally in the "home stretch." But I also felt profoundly grateful we *had* come so far together.

Hope in the Analyst

I believe that the analyst's hopefulness is partially the product of intense personal conviction. To be genuinely hopeful, the analyst must be sure she would do everything possible to further the treatment. That sense of willingness to go the "extra mile" engenders the analyst's hope. Certainty that she can expend effort beyond the "reasonable" maintains hope, because "reasonable" efforts may have already been made, without much effect. Knowing she is willing to go further than that allows her to sustain optimism. She can have realistic hope because she can count on herself to do whatever the treatment takes.

Thus the analyst's hope is not a form of naïveté and is not without foundation. It is a product of fierce determination. Like a parent with the conviction that he would do anything for his child, if the analyst knows nothing can stop him, he has a good reason to hope. The analyst's hopefulness is really a form of self-knowledge.

Frieda Fromm-Reichmann (Hornstein, 2000) was a great example of therapeutic determination:

> She was willing to try practically anything that might help them, which was a great deal more than most other psychiatrists were willing to do. She saw one patient at ten o'clock at night because that's when she was most likely to talk. She took others on walks around hospital grounds, or to symphony concerts, or to country inns for lunch. Those too distraught to leave at the end of an hour were permitted to stay for two. If a patient was violent and couldn't be let off the ward, she went to his room or saw him in restraints, if necessary. "She would have swung from the chandelier like Tarzan if she thought it would help," Joanne Greenberg later observed. A colleague remarked, not admiringly, that Frieda's patients got better because she simply gave them no other choice [pp. xv–xvi].

The analyst maintains her own hope through indefatigable effort. This both centers us and pushes us forward. We are centered in our absolute determination. This defines us to ourselves, but also exhorts us to fight for the treatment.

In a sense, the analyst's emotional position can be likened to Job's. Slochower (1970) points out that Job's strength comes from his steady belief that his love of God would be manifested throughout his trials (p. 55).

So far my clinical experience persuades me that

1. Hope has an interpersonal aspect, in that it can partially be a gift one person gives another, who may exist in reality, fantasy, or memory.
2. Hope is stronger when it is realistic, not based on an illusory sense of control over life.
3. Hope has within it self-knowledge about the strength of our own determination to accomplish something. If we will do anything a treatment requires, we have a greater basis for hope.

In treatment the task of inspiring hope is often initially the analyst's. We can recognize and work on emotional obstacles to hopefulness in ourselves, our supervisees, and our patients, but we cannot decide to hope or force another to hope.

Our own hopefulness is conveyed through our perseverance, even in the face of seeming stasis. A stubborn unwillingness to give up says a great deal. We also live hope through our resilience, our acceptance of difficulty, and our willingness to work hard, face pain, and confront ourselves honestly. These values are manifested in our conduct of a treatment. We reveal them in our tone, our focus, our stamina, and in so many other subtle ways. Those we have known personally and professionally can become part of what I call the "internal chorus" that the analyst calls on to sustain her hope and inspire her to be able to elicit it in the patient.

Coltart (1993) has described what is necessary for the analyst to maintain hope:

> Our faith as therapists, that what we are doing is eminently worth doing, day by day, without memory and without desire, is only one of its (faith's) manifestations. Yet it may well be our most precious possession, for without it I fear we would often be lost in confusion, not-knowing, or despair in our long, drawn-out relationships with people who are unhappy and who put a truly awesome trust-faith-in us to help them through their dark nights of the soul [p. 107].

Stephen Mitchell, whose death has brought us all great pain, also profoundly contributed to our lives through his remarkable insight. In his book *Hope and Dread in Psychoanalysis,* Mitchell (1993) addresses the analyst's hopes:

> We tend not to speak or write much of the analyst's hopes as such, because that sounds too personal somehow. The analyst is portrayed as professional, providing a generic service that helps when applied properly. But we all know that it is much more personal than that, that the analyst's hopes for her patient are embedded in and deeply entangled with her own sense of herself, her worth, what she can offer, what she has found deeply meaningful in her own life. The more we have explored the complexities of countertransference, the more we have come to realize how personal a stake the analyst inevitably has

in the proceedings. It is important to be able to help; it makes us anxious when we are prevented from helping or do not know how to help. Our hopes for the patient are inextricably bound up with our hopes for ourselves [pp. 207–208].

Mitchell's work, in part, prompted me (Buechler, 1995b, 2002a) to write about how I believe the analyst can evoke the patient's hope:

The aspect of active hope that affirms a commitment to life is probably not generally communicated in the content of what is said but, rather, in the fervor of the tone, in the strength of conviction that may be signaled by directness and forceful-ness of speech. In analysis, this is probably conveyed to the pa-tient more fully by personal and professional attitudes the analyst reveals unwittingly. Love of the work, a passion for promoting life and growth, an empathic stance toward herself and others, a willingness to struggle, joy in the humor and challenge of life are some of the intangibles that make them-selves known in the subtle timing and gestures of the music, rather than in the words. What the analyst focuses on, re-sponds to, is willing to break the frame for, lets pass in silence, meets with passion, expresses in the first person, tires about, is willing to fight, says a great deal. The same can be said in su-pervision, where the supervisor's and the supervisee's atti-tudes about treatment and life are often explicitly, as well as implicitly, studied [1995b, pp. 72–73].

One of the ways I believe we engender hope is by encouraging ex-perimentation with life. In an interesting footnote, Zeddies (2002) remarks,

Many patients come for treatment with a very restricted range of possibilities of who they are or who they can be. Part of the work, as some writers have emphasized (e.g., Mitchell, 1993; Cooper, 2000) involves reinvigorating and sustaining hope that it is worth the risk to try out or experiment with different ways of being in the world that might offer a better, more loving, richer, and more satisfying way of life than they have previously allowed themselves to envision [p. 430].

But I don't think we can foster an experimental attitude without demonstrating it. Thus, when we encourage a patient who has never traveled to try it, we are experimenting with technique, just as we are inviting the patient to experiment with life. We are manifesting hopefulness about venturing. Rather than taking a safer approach, we are risking our own position and going out on a limb. In this example, we could focus on courage or curiosity (in both analyst and patient) as well as spirited hope.

At first this deliberate departure from neutrality may sound extreme, but I think it is less novel than it seems. A 50-year-old patient says, "I've never been out of the country." Anything that comes next expresses the analyst's stance, including saying nothing. Any response indicates about what the analyst is and is not willing to take an explicit position on. Depending on the tone and inflection, even a simple "Oh" can say to the patient, "We should be looking at this as a problem. I hope to get you to be less fearful about travel in the future." More explicit encouragement to try something new and see what it is like, adds open advocation of new experience—for itself and for what can be learned about the patient's fears by encountering and countering them. Willingness to learn from new experience is embedded in Sullivan's (1953, 1954) notion of emotional health. Our choice is not whether to advocate for experimenting with life, but rather how openly, how actively, how passionately to do so. I believe that the more definitive position embodies and inspires hope more effectively.

I understand that this may tilt the vital balance (Greenberg, 1991) between being an old (transferential) versus a new object. We are more in danger of losing the power to evoke transference reactions the more we are new experiences for the patient. And other dangers exist, such as the question of maintaining professional boundaries, the question of which new experiences to encourage, and, more generally, whether the analyst has any privileged knowledge of a psychologically healthy way to live life. These are extremely serious issues, deserving much more attention than I can give them here. But I believe that by embracing experimentation, we gain the chance to promote clearly a hopeful, playful stance on life. If the ability to profit from new experience is what promotes growth (including insight about old behavioral patterns), openly advocating experimentation is worth the risks it entails.

The idea that promoting hope requires being more of a new than an old object is implicit in Shaw's (2003) conception of analytic love:

If the analysand's vitality and authenticity potentials were thwarted in the course of development, he has a second chance to realize those potentials with the analyst. The analyst's love and respect for the potential in a human being serves to encourage analysands whose experiences of deprivation of love, or of love without sufficient respect, have been overwhelmingly discouraging [p. 268].

Later Shaw directly connects the analyst's own hopes for the patient with the growth of analytic love:

We sustain our analytic purpose with even the most difficult of analysands because we hope that they will get better. We hope that what we provide will bear fruit in the analysand's life, in the form of his healing and growth. Very often, witnessing the fruits of our labor in the form of the analysand's newfound trust, and hard-earned healing and growth evokes and further stimulates our loving feelings [p. 268].

The analyst can be a catalyst for hope when he is comfortable with having influence on the patient (Mitchell, 1997; S. H. Cooper, 2000). Comfort with having an impact is, I believe, a prerequisite for the analyst. The analyst who is afraid of his impact or who feels guilty about it cannot fight passionately for life. Carefulness pulls him to pass up chances to elicit hope. When Joanne Greenberg (quoted earlier in Hornstein, 2000) said Fromm-Reichmann would have swung from the chandelier if she thought it would help, she was not describing an analyst afraid to have an impact. She was describing someone willing to do *anything* to help the patient see that life is worth fighting for.

The current intersubjective climate has probably affected the analyst's hopes more than the patient's. Patients continue to hope for improvements in the quality of their life experience. Our theoretical advances have no impact on patients' unabating desire to feel more joy and suffer less anxiety and depression. In hospital-based treatments, both participants have probably not changed their hopes to any great extent. The clinician in that setting still wants to enable the patient to live "on the outside." What has changed most, I would suggest, is the analyst's hopes in his private practice, but even there the changes are (or should be) limited. Freud's oft-quoted hopeful expectation was to reduce neurotic suffering to "common human misery." How would today's intersubjective outlook change this hope? Because we believe in a coconstructed reality, we aren't satisfied to hope for so little. Freud assumed the patient's reality is invariant, but he hoped treatment would alter *how the patient experiences his reality.* Neurotic suffering was a distorted response to a reality that objectively only warranted a response of common human misery. Analysis, Freud hoped, would help the patient's reactions better fit current reality.

For us today, "reality" is not uncovered (Freud) or corrected (of its parataxic distortions, Sullivan). Reality is coconstructed. Thus the analyst can hope for the patient to actually create a healthier reality, not just respond better to it. The sky is the limit! We have arrived at an analytic version of the American Wild West. Uncertainty is the untamed, unlimited frontier. We no longer hope for something as circumscribed as the patient's recognition of the oedipal derivation of his suffering. Today analytic adventurers and their patients don't know where they are going until they get there. The analyst in this uncharted territory thus can hope for anything (and be endlessly disappointed).

The patient, however, is still anchored to her life. She wants to feel better tomorrow than she did yesterday. She still hopes for more joy, zest, and love and less depression, rage, loneliness, and pain. Embracing uncertainty and paradox has brought analysts a vital aliveness but has also, perhaps, distended our hopes too much. We have to find a compromise that preserves this vitality and openness but satisfies patients' needs for the treatment to address clearly their emotional experience. I spell out in later chapters how attention to the balance of emotions can help us forge that compromise.

Galvanizing Hope

One of the reasons hope is so hard to define is that we don't always differentiate enough the driving emotion of hope from an expectant state of mind. Emotional hope pushes us to move forward. Wishfulness is a less directed, less driven, more cognitive than emotional state of expectation.

Analysts have sometimes equated hope with its cognitive aspect, as a favorable expectation. This seems to be what Sullivan, for example, is referring to when he says that the patient must "expect to derive benefit" from every session in order to participate in the work (1954, p. 4). Cognitive hope is the wishful expectation that things will change for the better in the future. This cognitive expectation is amenable to insightful interpretation. The patient who sees that her expectations, which have been based on past experience, have not adequately registered present circumstances, may begin to hope. Consider, for example, a patient who was humiliated by her father when she showed she wanted something very much. She came to expect humiliation for expressing strong desire. But this connection, and even the expectation itself, was not immediately available to her awareness. Like the proverbial fish who was the last one to know of water, she was unaware of her most fundamental assumptions and their experiential basis. In treatment she had to see what she automatically expected (humiliation for expressing desire) and why (repeated experiences with her father) before she could recognize that her present situation was different, and she could hope for better responses to her desire in the future.

Cognitive hope is enormously helpful, but it is often not enough to sustain treatment. An active, galvanizing, emotional hope is also necessary. But where does that push toward life come from?

Schachtel (1959) emphasizes hope's role as a galvanizing emotion, and not just a cognitive expectation. He supplies an entire framework for the study of the emotions and distinguishes embeddedness affects, which strive toward tension reduction, from the activity affects, our more eager, directed emotional experiences. Schachtel calls the hopeful activity affect "realistic hope." He believes that in realistic hope the present is not experienced as a desert through which one has to wander to arrive at the future. It receives significance from the activities that make one's life meaningful or through which one tries to help bring about hoped-for change. Although realistic hope, too, is directed toward the future, it does not shift the emphasis from the present to anticipation of the future (p. 39).

Thus we have a contrast between a cognitive hopeful expectation of something in the future and an emotional striving that gratifies in the present, as it prepares for the future. Behavior that is motivated by hope as an activity affect should be gratifying both as a means to an end and as an end in itself.

Erich Fromm (1973, quoted in Hornstein, 2000, p. 390) captured the activating nature of the emotion of hope:

> To have faith means to dare, to think the unthinkable, yet to act within the limits of the realistically possible; it is the paradox of hope to expect the Messiah every day, yet not to lose heart when

he has not come at the appointed hour. This hope is not passive
and it is not patient; on the contrary, it is impatient and active,
looking for every possibility of action within the realm of real
possibilities.

Realistic hope often requires embracing paradox. A patient asks
why he should believe therapy can help him when he is still depressed after many years of treatment. For both of us, maintaining our hope requires truly accepting the paradoxical nature of life. To me, hope means
to have the humility to understand that my senses and logic can mislead
me. The unalterable may change. Hard work can refresh. Accepting a
patient's profound despair may help lift it, because then, at least, he is
not alone. It is possible to hope emotionally in the absence of high expectations if the interpersonal context inspires it. Inspiring enough hope is
one of our central tasks. Menninger (1959) put this in the form of a challenge: "It is a responsibility of the teacher to the student, just as it is of the
young doctor to his patient, to inspire the right amount of hope—some,
but not too much. Excess of hope is presumption and leads to disaster.
Deficiency of hope is despair and leads to decay" (p. 4).

Like all other human emotions, hope cannot be understood outside the context of the other emotions it joins (Buechler, 1993,
1995a). The emotions form a system in the human being (Izard, 1977)
with the experience and expression of each modified by the levels of
all the others. We cannot speak of our hopes without reference to
what is, or is not, providing joy and what is, or is not eliciting shame,
anxiety, anger. Hope is shaped partially by avid curiosity and partially by the capacity to be surprised. As an emotion, hope is modified
by the other motivating forces it accompanies.

Thus in Schachtel's (1959) language, we could probably predict the
strength of the embeddedness affect of hope from knowing the degree
of certainty of the individual's expectations, for this type of hope is
close to a cognitive appraisal. But to understand the motivating, activ-
ity-inspiring power of hope, we need to look beyond expectations, regardless of their certainty, to a complex array of other emotions and
attitudes that shape these forces.

I understand this hope as an anchor, centering us in ourselves, re-
quiring the willing embrace of life's essential paradoxes. As analysts it
requires us to be steeped in the knowledge of our good intentions. We
must candidly, forthrightly face our personal stake in our work, without too much shame or guilt, although knowing that retrospect will

sometimes show our efforts to have been inadequate or misdirected. Nevertheless, through our faces, tones, and unyielding efforts we must demonstrate passionate concern for life. We must understand and convey to our patients the truly paradoxical nature of hope. Sometimes we have to let go of all specific hopes to hold on to its essence. Sometimes hope requires the humility to know that we are not yet ready to conceive the shape of things to come.

But I would say that analyst and patient each bring something vital, but different, to the task of conceiving the future. Pizer (1998) puts it this way:

> I believe in the necessarily steady asymmetry of the analyst's and the patient's different roles in the treatment relationship and clinical process—the distinct responsibilities and exposures that both must bring to their respective jobs in the joint task. Yet, I would radically state the mutuality, and spirit, of analytic negotiation in these terms: we depend on each other [p. 206].

We do depend on each other, and we have different roles. The analyst brings sensitivity to "hope for the wrong thing." She has studied the many "wrong things" people hope for (e.g., narcissistic perfections, schizoid compromises, obsessional control). She is steeped in awareness of these human patterns, having encountered them in herself and many others. This is similar, in spirit, to Sullivan's conception of our role in discerning patterns of interpersonal relatedness. But when it comes to hope for the "right thing," the analyst has no superior knowledge. Patient and analyst equally collaborate in this part of the process. What emerges from their encounter is greater clarity (for both) about their particular ways of being a human being. As I elaborate in subsequent chapters this includes their personal approach to balancing emotions, facing life with courage, finding purpose, and bearing inevitable loss.

3   *Kindness in Treatment*

Still in training, I became embroiled in a very public disagreement with a senior faculty member. I poured out my troubles to my analyst, who at first mainly listened silently. Next session, she met me in the waiting room when I arrived. She said she wanted to take me to lunch, instead of holding our session. I can still remember my amazement. This was entirely different from anything that had transpired in our fairly traditional analytic work together. During lunch she explained that she had wanted a different setting to tell me that, considering the very significant issues at stake, she thought I was right in the position I was taking and should continue to voice my opinion.

After this "session" we resumed our usual routine, although we certainly did discuss the lunch, and the meaning of the situation to me. Roughly a quarter of a century has passed, and I believe this incident is still exerting a powerful effect on me. Why?

Of course this question can be addressed at various levels, and I am considering only the aspect relevant to treatment technique. I am sure that part of the incident's powerful impact stems from the fact that it so significantly differed from our usual frame. In this chapter, I discuss some of the sources of the vitality of the treatment process as I understand them. This topic is not unlike the issue of the "therapeutic action." I am, however, limiting the focus to a narrow band of the emotional countertransference (for more extensive exploration of therapeutic action, see Mitchell, 1988, pp. 278–306; Mitchell, 1997, chapter 2, pp. 33–62; Altman, 2002, pp. 499–513; D. B. Stern, 2002, pp. 515–525).

I have no doubt that, whatever else was involved, this was an act of kindness. My analyst knew I needed support. I think she must have given considerable thought about whether to break a frame she believed in. She died years ago, so I will never know whether she consciously meant to model something for me, as a budding analyst. But I do believe that, however conscious it was for her, she was showing me, as well as telling me, how to have the courage of my convictions.

Interestingly, the impact of this incident changes over the years as I reframe it. This is similar to how our own childhood experience acquires new meanings when we become parents. Considered in a new light, history morphs. At the time I was bolstered, deeply touched, and grateful. But her actions have more meaning for me now. I have studied and written about the concept of neutrality (Buechler, 1999). Everything I write, including this book, is, in a sense, about "therapeutic action." I believe in the value of using my own experience to understand these theoretical concepts.

Today, one shape this memory takes is as an example of how conviction is conveyed. It speaks to the issue of integrity, or wholeness (see chapter 8). It illustrates the effect of contrast. The frame is necessary partly to give departures from the frame meaning and power just as life's finiteness helps define it (Hoffman, 1998).

Whether I remember it as an analysand, analyst, supervisor, or teacher, this incident represents an act of kindness to me. I believe it took some thought, effort, and courage. Because the lessons I read from it multiply over the years, my gratitude grows. I consider it now a striking instance of a powerful therapeutic action that took the form of an "enactment" (see Renik, 1995; Mitchell, 1997, p. 128; D. B. Stern, 1997, pp. 248–249).

Perhaps I can bring out another facet of this experience. Part of its great effect stems from how easy it would have been for my analyst to justify refraining from taking this action. I was in analysis and learning to be an analyst, and this clearly broke our usual frame in many ways. She was, in a sense, playing a real role in my here-and-now experience. Much of the literature, certainly at that time, would have supported refraining. She was taking the harder, less traveled road, which I think makes her example more potent. Perhaps we can see her as "courting surprise" (D. B. Stern, 1990) by doing the unexpected.

I could also look at this incident as an act of faith in us as collaborators. She knew we could, and would, return to the frame. This aspect has more meaning for me now than when it happened. Frequently acts of simple kindness in treatment have their greatest impact years after they occur. At the end of a long treatment, patients will mention moments that seemed (to me) relatively trivial when they happened. But they are remembered long after the (conscious) memory of verbal interpretations has faded. Actions such as lending a patient an umbrella when a sudden storm arose, placing a patient's chair where she was most comfortable, actively working out the time and the fee to make treatment feasible, sharing information or countertransference when it might be useful—all these can be important. They would, of course, be relatively insignificant in other contexts, but in treatment they may contrast with the frame, which therefore highlights them. They mean more than they usually would when they occur in this context.

Perhaps some of the impact of such an act of kindness in treatment is that it satisfies the patient's craving to matter. It offers the patient a palpable demonstration that someone felt he was worth their extending themselves. However seemingly trivial, these moments can be palpable crystallizations of an ongoing kindness that usually shows itself more subtly. Focus on one aspect of the material, away from another, may be the clinician's most frequent act of kindness, but it is harder to discern and remember, because it isn't easily retained as a story. This nonnarrative element makes some kindness elusive, but overt actions are like lightposts, memorably illuminating the kindness at the heart of the process. A patient becomes confused, makes a slip of the tongue, and is clearly embarrassed. It is, I think, a simple act of kindness to say nothing. She heard the slip, so it may still be useful. But even if this means we make less use of the slip, it may be worth it. The priority it expresses is that people's feelings are more important than making points. This may be as much an act of kindness as, say, lending an umbrella, but it is much less clearly (consciously) remembered, because silence about the slip is the *absence* of a verbal exchange. It is less crystallized as a narrative event. Nevertheless, often on a less than conscious level, I believe these kindnesses can have great impact.

Before further considering kindness as part of the therapeutic action, I would like to explore briefly the related, but much broader, concept of enactment (see Bromberg, 1998, p. 23, for an interesting discussion of the contrast between enactments inside and outside of treatment). Because *enactment* is currently a highly overused term, it is important for me to be clear about exactly what it means to me.

The history of attitudes toward countertransference is being replayed in relation to "enactment." Early in the history of analysis, countertransference was an unfortunate event that the analyst could avoid if she was properly analyzed herself (Freud, 1910; Reich, 1951, 1960, 1966). Gradually, countertransference began to be seen as being at the work's core (Racker, 1968). There came a growing sense that it had many positive uses (Sandler, 1976; Epstein and Feiner, 1979). Its crucial importance to the treatment process is hardly disputed today.

The term *enactment* has had a similar history. At first an enactment was a living out, in treatment, of a significant aspect of the patient's psychic experience. Enactments are assumed to be unconscious for the patient, and often for the analyst. But, the analyst's conscious awareness of the enactment is supposed to grow to the point that he sees its meaning and can communicate that to the patient (for a discussion of how this occurs in Sullivanian vs. other treatment contexts, see Bromberg, 1998, p. 26).

Like countertransference, enactments by the analyst have gone from being unfortunate deviations, to being unfortunate regular occurrences, to being meaningful events, to being necessary and useful events (see Bromberg, 1998, chapter 11, pp. 147–165, for a discussion of some contrasting stances).

But even in our more tolerant view, some types of enactment receive more attention than others. We are probably more likely to see ourselves enacting a split with a particular patient than enacting a psychoanalytic ideal with all patients, which is what I am focusing on in this book. Enactments are taken as meaningful about our own and a particular patient's psychic functioning. This, although valid, should not, in my judgment be privileged over other aspects. My analyst asking me to lunch had, of course, meanings to me borne of my earlier life experience and psychic makeup. What we lived out together can, and should be seen as expressing our individual characters and earlier object relationships. But it also represents the manifestation of a value that has a more generalizable meaning in the psychoanalytic context. Treatment is not viable without some demonstrable kindness, at least on the part of the clinician toward the patient. Without some acts of kindness, treatment stalls or terminates. Although of course the patient may also be kind, I am focusing on the clinician's kindness.

Like curiosity, hope, courage, meaning, purpose, integrity, emotional balance, and the ability to bear loss, kindness is a treatment necessity. It may be commonplace, but its manifestation in an interchange does reflect the nexus of two particular personalities with specific life histories. It also reflects an essential treatment value lived out in countless sessions, between numberless patients and clinicians. Some forms of kindness may be more vital to work with a specific patient than others. Perhaps I especially needed the form my analyst and I enacted, for personal reasons. Perhaps she especially needed to manifest this form, for her own personal reasons, reflective of her personality and life experience. But individual differences in the form of expression aside, some kindness is a treatment necessity.

An analogy would be the expression of the fundamental emotions (Izard, 1977). All human beings express some form of anger, fear, sadness, and joy. In varying cultures, what triggers these emotions may differ. Individual personality and experience also affects what triggers each emotion and just how it is expressed. But some expression of anger, fear, sadness, and joy (and other emotions) is integral to being human. Analogously, what triggers expressions of hope, kindness, curiosity, courage, purpose, meaning, integrity, emotional balance, and the bearing of loss is different in each of us, and the expression of it also varies. But these values must be manifested in some way for a treatment to be viable.

In the remainder of this chapter, I consider some of the forms kindness takes in treatment. My focus on the clinician's kindness is not meant to minimize the meaningfulness of the patient's kindness. I concentrate on types of kindness that recur with great frequency in treatment contexts. Briefly, these kindnesses include the clinician's willing, temporary sacrifice of equanimity, cognitive and emotional functioning, and pride. Eventually the clinician has to be able to give up the patient, which is often, in some senses, a sacrifice. Interestingly, although treatment could not be viable without kindness, clinicians are often afraid to be kind. This fear is, in my view, an important obstacle in training. Some thoughts about this problem end the chapter.

Kindness expressed as sacrifice appears in countless literary forms. Shakespeare's *King Lear,* Rattigan's *In Praise of Love,* and Gorky's *Mother* can be seen as accounts of the development of the capacity to sacrifice. What I believe clinicians "know" but may not formulate (D. B. Stern, 1997) is that many treatment records are also stories of kind sacrifices.

An Unquiet Mind

The fundamental sacrifice clinicians make is the voluntary surrender of peace of mind (or the sacrifice of a piece of our minds). Another way to express this is to look at the sorrow, shame, guilt, regret, fear, loneliness, anxiety, anger, envy, and jealousy we bear for the sake of the patient's treatment.

Once a year I teach a seminar on emotions in psychotherapy. I have been amazed at the stories that come out of these meetings. Although all the participants know their experiences have been difficult, few formulate the pain they have endured as a type of sacrifice that eventually convinces the patient of their good intentions toward him. Therapists listen, day after day, to every imaginable human horror, largely unable to take direct action. For the most part we "contain." We are receptacles for human suffering. However we bear this entails a sacrifice. If we remain open and very responsive we can burn out, exhausting our empathy. But if we try to deaden ourselves to pain, we sacrifice even more.

A therapist listens, hour after hour, to experiences of political torture to help these victims live with the psychological legacy of what they have endured. Another clinician works with hospitalized psychotic patients and is subjected to the confusing gross inappropriateness, harsh intensity, sheer dangerousness, and dingy desperation of that world. A third who treats children listens helplessly to stories of chilling abuse too subtle to qualify for protective services. Often she has to choose between anxiously reporting the abuse (risking loss of the parents' collaboration, and, perhaps, losing the chance to work with the child) versus a guilty silence, bracing for the possibility of even greater harm to the child. If she chooses silence, she also bears the possibility that, should the abuse escalate, her silence will be found out and judged negligent. Whichever set of risks she chooses to take, she will probably feel alone with something hard to bear. This loneliness is the sense of isolation with one's point of view. No one experiences the situation exactly as she does.

A fourth clinician, a mental health liaison, works with the elderly. His daily schedule includes a spectrum of loss—loss of health, sanity, dignity. At 10 o'clock he might talk to a son describing the slow, steady mental deterioration of his father who has Alzheimer's—a father who no longer recognizes him. At 11 o'clock he might talk to a recent widow about the loss of her life's companion. I am sure he benefits from this work in many ways, but I am equally certain it entails very real sacrifices.

Another way to say this is that the clinician in private practice, or in other settings, forfeits something absolutely necessary. Human beings need time to recover from a shock (Pearlman and Saakitne, 1995; van der Kolk, 1995). Often the vicarious pain we feel can jolt us into intense awareness of the fragility of the human condition. Clinicians expect themselves to move on, every hour, to the next jolt with no time or attention to our own recovery process. Like some kind of Pavlovian caricature we are supposed to respond to the buzzer that announces the next patient. We feel, rightly, that this person also deserves our full attention and emotional availability. But what do we sacrifice in trying to provide this availability?

I think that the effort to shift gears constantly is the greatest sacrifice we make for our patients because it is also the most costly. It is a silent gift, often unnoticed by both participants. But with the years of springing back, hour after hour, we are likely to lose elasticity.

For example, I spend 45 minutes listening to a patient's pain about the death of the one truly caring parent figure she ever knew. The patient's effort to feel her loss fully and bear it with dignity moves me. During the hour with her I strive for something similar. I try to maintain touch with myself, to glean what I can, and give her the fruits of my immersion. The session ends with the arrival of the next patient, who storms into my office, in a rage at the boss she feels is abusing his power.

This is a very ordinary sequence of events in the life of a clinician. Even if my schedule included more rest periods, I can't know in advance when I will most need one. I might still end up with no time to consider my response to the bereaved patient, absorb its meaning about me, accept what it says to me about life, consider reframings that might help me recover. I have to surrender to the feelings the first patient evokes, then distance enough from them to learn something (my version of Sullivan's, 1954, participant-observation). With the arrival of the next patient I have to let go instantly of this set of affects and associated thoughts. The image of a tennis player comes to mind, the position of one play leaving her off balance for the next.

To give myself to the next hour requires me to shift gears rapidly, opening myself to a very different set of affects. I must not let lingering feelings from the last hour obscure my experience of the present moment. I must sacrifice my teetering emotional balance yet again.

I might have just been finding my bearings. I have to let go of that, perhaps hard-won, triumph. Moving on is, I feel, the greatest sacrifice we make because in doing so we have to leave ourselves behind. I miss that precious moment that, extended, might have given me greater self-awareness, or at least peace.

Losing My Mind

Cognitive disruption as part of the ongoing experience of the clinician is well documented. The literature on countertransference (Epstein and Feiner, 1983; Wolstein, 1987; Ehrenberg, 1992; Hirsch, 1995) and on working with borderline patients (Stone, 1986; Sherby, 1989; Youngerman, 1995) suggests how the process can fragment the analyst. In biographies and autobiographies (Grosskurth, 1986; Dupont, 1988) the cognitive impact of the work is sometimes a central focus, at other times merely a sad footnote. But these stories are not generally framed as tales of the *sacrifice* of mental functioning. Yet that description often seems apt to me.

Take, for example, the case of "Jane" reported by Bollas in *The Shadow of the Object* (1987, pp. 226–227). I quote this poignant story at some length:

> I have written about some features of my countertransference with Jane (see chapter 11), particularly my awareness that early on in her therapy I tended just to look at her rather than listen to her. . . .
>
> Often her actions in any one session were so unpredictable, her moods so varying, that I never had a sense of where she was . . .
>
> Such was her expertise at distressing people that I gather that her previous therapist was greatly relieved when Jane left the analysis, and the highly skilled and experienced psychiatrist who provides me with mental cover telephoned me immediately after seeing her, informing me she was not at all sure that she could provide psychiatric cover since she found her extremely upsetting.
>
> For quite some time I was interpretively firm. I would concentrate on how she felt she could only communicate with someone if she could coerce him. Whenever she was attempting

this with me (which was almost constantly), I would calmly inform her of what I thought she was doing. Although this did settle her a little, and eventually became the bread and butter of our work, I was nonetheless aware that personally I found her traumatizing and that I had withdrawn from my more ordinary analytical self, hiding somewhat behind a classical stance. I would often privately regret having her as a patient and would think of a way to get rid of her: maybe she would move away or become disillusioned with me and want to go to someone else; or, if I was lucky, she would have a real breakdown, and the hospital would take her off my hands. I thought I would have to tell her that unfortunately I was unable to continue with her, that private practice has its limits, and so forth. I knew, however, that these feelings were the emergence of her primary objects. Clearly I was beginning to become the outline of the mother who was rid of her when she was a small child, and my fortitude in sticking my ground, interpreting the transference, and placing her idiom in a genetic reconstruction began to have some effect, and—to my disappointment, I can now confess—she felt I was helping her.

With Jane, Bollas couldn't think or feel, and he clearly lost the positive sense of himself as a clinician with therapeutic intentions. The latter portion of this quotation illustrates how our theoretical stance can help us bear doing treatment (see chapter 9 for a more extensive discussion of this). Briefly, because Bollas believes he *should* be inhabited by the patient's objects, he is less distressed than other clinicians might be in a similar situation. He feels like a kind of unhappy host, temporarily housing an unpleasant guest he hopes will not stay too long. Yet he believes the evidence of his becoming like the patient's mother shows he is doing his job, rather than that he is losing his mind, his heart, or his identity (partly). What this means to me is that because of our theoretical differences Bollas and I would make different sacrifices with Jane. Bollas lost some peace of mind, cognitive and affective functioning, aliveness and centeredness. For me, I would experience wanting to be rid of Jane as *my* desire (*not* her mother's desire projected into me). Given my character, I might feel shame, guilt, or anxiety about this, as well as some measure of surprise. I don't generally feel such desire to be rid of a patient. Because, for me, it is *my* desire and therefore emanates from who I am as a human being, it can challenge how I think of myself as a clinician. To the extent that it violates my self-concept, it will surprise me and may evoke my guilt for not living up to my own standards of therapeutic conduct. It could threaten my sense of clinical adequacy, and therefore shame me. The potential for exposure might make me anxious.

But there are also important similarities in what Bollas and I would bear with Jane as our patient. Not being able to think or feel is a powerful experience, a potentially traumatic paralysis. While Bollas and I might differ in whom we hold responsible, both of us would miss our accustomed self-experience. Each of us might feel lonely, with no one with whom we could share our reactions. We might feel confused by our strange and unbidden feelings. With Jane both Bollas and I forfeit familiar selves, Bollas to function as a receptacle for impressions, like a wax stamp softly molded into new shapes. I might complain of feeling "not myself" with Jane and yearn for the safety of an easier patient. After a day filled with "Janes" I may have to modify my clinical self-concept more than Bollas, but both of us would have lived through many intensely alienated hours.

Being a Fool for Love

One of the clinician's most frequent, significant sacrifices is her pride. The vast literature on countertransference disclosure (Blechner, 1992; Hirsch, 1995; Maroda, 1999) can be read as a history of the effort to "go first" in exposing ourselves. Implicitly it is not unlike the childhood bargain that "I'll show you mine, if you'll show me yours." Without conceptualizing it this way, I feel we offer up our own pride and create an atmosphere that will be conducive for the patient to reveal himself by being willingly self-revealing.

I call the clinician's sacrifice of pride being a "fool for love," and I see it as most relevant to the treatment of narcissism (see chapter 5 for a fuller discussion of this).

Examples of clinicians' willing self-exposure include Blechner's discussion, with a patient, of his own dream (Blechner, 2001). Maroda's (1999, 2002) extensive published case material abounds with illustrations of her exposure of emotional responses. Ehrenberg (1992) has also provided many relevant vignettes. The work of Mitchell (1993, 1997) underscores the potential therapeutic value of the clinician's openness. Renik's (1998) concept of self-revealing can be understood, from this perspective, as effective not so much for what he discloses to the patient, as for the values he is enacting by being willing to self-expose.

From this vantage point we can dialogue with current trends in the interpersonal and relational literature, agreeing as to what is effective but differing as to *why* it is effective: regardless of the reasons for disclosure in the mind of the analyst, what most affects the patient is that by disclosing the analyst expresses his priorities. When we offer to tell the patient our experience, we are taking a position about what counts most in life. We are manifesting the valuing of health over pride, of having impact over remaining comfortable. We are announcing who we would like to be and what we are trying hardest to do.

Among myriad instances of this, I briefly consider the work of Coen (2002). In the clinical material that suffuses his writing, he supplies countless examples of sharing his experience. What makes them effective is not so much their content, but rather the values he is manifesting. To make this point I could quote much of the book, but I will let the following vignette suffice (pp. 68–69):

> The previous day we had again gone through his destruction of meaning and value of the treatment. Once more he insisted he should end the treatment, and I felt tempted to agree with him. But, as we were able to talk about his destroying anything good between us, he could join me collaboratively in reflecting on what he had done to our relationship. The next day, in trying to engage him about what he'd missed as a child and now needed, I told him about my brief "talk" the previous evening on the telephone with my two-year-old grandson in another city. I said it was very sad that my grandson regularly could expect to get what Mr. N. had gotten so little of—parents, or me as grandparent, enjoying and admiring him, in this example, my grandson's beginning ability to exchange a few words on the telephone with me. Mr. N. was touched both by my example and by my sharing my experience with him. He was especially touched that I did not remain angry and rejecting of him for how dismissive he had been with me the previous day.

I would suggest it is not so much what Coen shared but the values he expressed by choosing to share that had significant therapeutic impact.

I think of this as a corollary of the limited impact of insight. Just as the patient's self-knowledge can only go so far in helping him effect change, so the content of the clinician's self-exposure matters less than the values embodied in the telling.

Termination as Sacrifice

In supervision I hear about a relatively lengthy and intense psychotherapy. The patient has made strides to modify a reclusive schizoid isolation and an obsessional rigidity. For the first time in his life, he has a few friends he sees regularly. His career has ended, successfully, and an early retirement offers him a comfortable lifestyle. He has seen his mother through her last illness with attentiveness. This protects him from some regrets, although he does still painfully miss her. He brings up the question of terminating his treatment, posing it in positive terms, as something he feels ready for.

His therapist acknowledges her dilemma to me. Years of work with this patient have taught her that it is his style to find ways to delimit intimacy. Essentially this was his presenting problem at the outset of the treatment. Progress has been made, but he is not in a committed relationship and has a limited social life, although it is richer than before treatment. She is happy to acknowledge his gains, yet disconcerted by the thought of termination. Why? Is this pure self-interest, reluctance to accept the loss of income, or of *her* attachment to him? Or is she intuitively sensing one more schizoid maneuver in a patient still prone to avoid intimacy? Because he may terminate regardless of her stance, should she embrace it graciously, to validate his sense of accomplishment? Or should she hold out for further growth?

This is the kind of dilemma that clearly highlights the role of our values in doing treatment. Given that there is no clear-cut right answer, which priorities (about treatment, mental health, relationships, life) should we each bring to these complicated judgment calls?

Subtle interpersonal negotiations (Pizer, 1998) often preoccupy treatments toward their end. Even when neither participant consciously notices it, there may be many hidden agendas expressed in the topics raised and those ignored. Focusing on areas in which the work is incomplete can communicate the message that the treatment should continue.

Although there is no definitely right response, in this situation I felt it was more right than wrong for the therapist to accept termination willingly. This is not because the clinician's self-interest would be served if treatment continued. It is, for me, purely a matter of priorities. What seemed to me to be therapeutically most important was sending this schizoid man a clear signal that was markedly non-schizoid in the priorities it expressed. I felt it should be made exceptionally clear that his therapist was unwilling to go through the motions of prolonging the work. Especially with such a patient it might be easy to hold on to a routinized, unalive treatment. No matter how reasonably such a stance can be justified, it fails to contrast vividly enough with the patient's schizoid compromises.

Ending proved difficult. A kind of entropy exerted a powerful pull toward continuing the treatment. For one thing, there are no established rites. There is no funeral for defunct treatments. Official divorce is impossible, even when there is flagrant incompatibility. In this instance the sense of loss was especially hard to process (see chapter 7 for a more extended discussion of the experience of loss at termination; here I only consider the part sacrifice plays). The therapist felt inhibited about expressing her feelings of loss to the patient because she was concerned that even this would be experienced as an attempt to coerce him to stay. Loss became the elephant in the room. While it couldn't be addressed, it was so big that it crowded out everything else.

Not enough, in my opinion is written about termination's impact on the clinician (exceptions include Coltart, 1993; Hoffman, 1998; Buechler, 2000; and Coen, 2002). Ours is the only profession that requires the *total* discontinuance of contact. Former pupils can surprise their old teachers with a call or a visit. Adult offspring still visit their parents, giving each a changed, but still vital, role in each others' lives. Friendships are theoretically possible with former accountants, dentists, veterinarians. Elsewhere (2003) I have argued that we should *never* develop a friendship with a former patient. It is not, in my judgment, enough to wait a prescribed period of time. It is always conceivable that a former patient could want to go back to a previous therapist for further treatment. This is precluded if they have become friends.

Thus, it is partially because there is no "tomorrow" that termination is so difficult. Clinicians face the complete loss of someone they intimately knew. I believe their acceptance of this loss is often a sacrifice made out of kindness, courage, integrity, and love. In an act analogous to parental encouragement to branch out from the "nest," the therapist is not just sacrificing an ongoing relationship. She knows she may never hear from this person again. Their story may never conclude, for her. Its ragged edge may trouble her, but there is nothing she can do about it.

The clinician has lost more than just the patient. She has lost peace of mind. Even if she comes to a belated certainty that termination was a mistake she can do nothing to rectify it and resume the relationship. Her only steady companion is uncertainty (Hoffman, 1987; McCleary, 1992; D. B. Stern, 1997). Termination often takes courage for both participants but, I believe, quite frequently it is a meaningful sacrifice for the clinician.

For the sake of brevity, at this point I merely list some of what I see as the acts of kindness and sacrifice clinicians frequently make. I have addressed some of them in this chapter. For the rest I offer here a brief description:

1. Clinicians often choose to work in situations in which they will be exposed to vicarious traumatizations.

2. Therapists take responsibility for an unremittingly endless series of judgment calls, with unknowable consequences at the time they are made.

3. Through terminations of one kind or another, therapists have to accept eventually losing every treatment relationship.

4. Therapists often bear intense loneliness without having the relaxation of being alone.

5. Clinicians live with constant uncertainty, paradox, and surprise.

6. We often have to forgo having time to process what happened during the last hour when the next patient arrives.

7. We often willingly expose our own shortcomings, especially in training (Buechler, 1992), even though it can hurt our pride.

8. While conducting treatment, we expose ourselves to feeling "on the spot," needing to think fast.

9. Clinicians are often pressed to be more psychologically available. Requests for more time, more empathy, more self-disclosure are common. We have to titrate giving of ourselves and live with the internal impact of our choices, as well as the impact on our patients.

10. Doing treatment faces us with aspects of ourselves we might prefer to ignore (deny, repress, etc.). In a Sullivanian (1953) sense, the analyst's "not me" sphere is often challenged.

11. What we literally have to sit with can be painful. That is, our freedom to move physically is limited, while simultaneously we may be intensely emotionally stirred. I have often wondered about the long-term physical and emotional effects on the clinician of the combination of a still body and an "unquiet" mind and heart.

12. We may not feel comfortable commenting on some of the contrasts we experience. Even when we are talking with colleagues, we may not be able to disclose certain information. This may mean there are aspects of our day we can share with no one. By "contrasts" I mean, for example, my sixth patient of the day may be trying to bear the loss of a child, while the seventh may be concerned about something that to me is trivial. Or I may, in my own life, be struggling with something that seems vastly different, or bigger, or not relevant to the work with a patient. For different reasons I may not be able to voice these contrasts to anyone.

13. We often have to live with "cognition interruptus." That is, we have a constant flow of unfinished, interrupted thought processes. From day to day, we carry fragments of feelingful thoughts. Sometimes they accumulate, snowball-fashion, or they may fracture our attention into tiny shards.

14. We have to be prepared to be treated unfairly, all day. We can expect to pay for the "sins of the father" (and not only our own fathers, but everyone else's!). We can't complain about the existence of the transference. We assented to being subjected to it, by coming to work.

15. We live with disparate injunctions all the time. We try, for example, to be enough of an "old object" to evoke the transference, but we also try to be "new objects," to foster new interpersonal experiences (Greenberg, 1991).

16. We hold many secrets.

17. Clinicians must bear being misconstrued. All human beings have to deal with the gap between our intentions and our effects but, as clinicians, I think we have to deal with this more often. We can't always defend ourselves (without being defensive or overly self-revealing or self-involved or leaving insufficient room for the patient's aggression).

18. We are "insiders" in many people's lives, and also "outsiders." We have no clear role at many of life's rituals, for example. Should we attend a patient's funeral? I once did so, only to learn there was no one there I could talk to, no one who really wanted to talk to me. I felt more alone than if I hadn't attended.

19. We must be relatively comfortable with conflicts of interest. The best fee policy for me isn't optimal for my patients, and so on.

20. Clinicians have to be capable of bearing regret. There is always an array of roads not taken in any treatment. Ultimately we are responsible for our focus and for what we end up neglecting.

Teaching Kindness

For treatment to be vitally alive, we have to "court surprise" (D. B. Stern, 1990) and "cultivate the improvisational" (Ringstrom, 2001). Some (not all) of treatment's most important surprises and improvisations (like my analyst's invitation to lunch) are also acts of kindness. Often they implicitly declare a set of priorities. I believe my analyst was letting me know that some things are so important to convey that we may have to invent a form for them.

I don't think improvisation can be taught without modeling it. But, even then, how can we teach people to think of lending a patient an umbrella? To be meaningful, it would have to be a real response to a particular moment. Despite our difficulty capturing and teaching kindness, we know it may have as much impact as any of the techniques we *do* try to teach.

I find that the pivotal obstacle to developing an easy kindness is the profession's wary silence on this subject. Perhaps it seems too commonplace to discuss kindness, or overly simplistic, or old-fashioned, or threatening to the maintenance of the frame, or nonintellectual. Perhaps some of us worry that being kind will take away what differentiates treatment from friendship or other relationships. But that does not negate the importance of being kind and showing genuine good will toward the patient. Kindness is as essential to treatment as curiosity, hope, courage, purpose, integrity, the ability to bear loss, and emotional balance. Although we can't teach clinicians exactly how to be kind, or when, we can affirm its significance and rescue it from its taboo status at conferences and training programs. For the good of a treatment, clinicians kindly sacrifice their peace of mind and heart, and their pride. Each clinician must find a personally comfortable, graceful way to make these offerings.

4   *Promoting Courage*

Both patient and therapist are in their 30s, but there the resemblance seems to end. The patient brings an intense Latin culture into the room, whereas the therapist is all shy reserve. As a writer the patient dwells on vivid descriptions of the obscenely violent. The therapist's language contains, reasons, clarifies.

The patient hasn't always been able to hold himself together. One time, when his mind unhinged, he had to be hospitalized. Hell had become too real, too present. It was no longer an imaginative setting for his writing. It had become a concrete place of residence.

When they talk about his childhood neglect and physical abuse, the therapist knows she can maintain her role. Familiar feelings of empathy, sorrow, and outrage accompany her as she explores his childhood victimization. In the present tense, however, she is less sure of herself with this edgy man and his wild, sinister imagination. Where is the line between therapeutic exploration of his fantasies and nontherapeutic seduction? Will he misinterpret her empathy and concern as a different sort of interest? And if he remembers too much, too fast, will he slip back into a permanent hell?

Even on his best days he inhabits a frightening world. In his mind's eye he sees dangerous, violent men and sexually starved, predatory women. Characters in his stories suffer bizarre fates, their lives taken over by alien forces.

Just as his story characters threaten to become too real, everyday life can assume a bizarre quality. A trip to the dentist becomes an ordeal, anxiety centered on the "torment" of not knowing what will be pulled from his mouth.

So what does the therapist say when the danger of the patient's decompensation seems very real? What does she say when his fantastic imaginary characters repulse or frighten *her?* When the stories of willing submission to sadism leave her wondering just how far this patient's acting out might go?

In short, how does the therapist deal with her own sense of potential danger? How does she bear the risks that the patient may:

1. Decompensate, perhaps especially when faced with disturbing memories of his childhood traumas.
2. Try to act out some of the sadomasochistic themes with the therapist or others.
3. Use the treatment, and a growing love for the therapist, in place of a life outside treatment.
4. Remain stuck, forever, boldly fantasizing inwardly but living a barren existence in the outer world.

It all depends on whether the therapist has enough courage and can promote courage in the patient. Ultimately courage counts for more than any insight. It takes courage to face the risks of this work unflinchingly. I have come to believe it takes a great deal of courage to be a clinician, even with less challenging patients than this one. A therapist's ordinary day can be filled with difficult human questions about illness, aging, financial worries, family conflicts, and so on. Whatever troubles us personally is bound to come up in our work. When we sit across from a patient, we open ourselves to having to recognize all kinds of human vulnerabilities. The layperson might have the luxury of defensively focusing away from some issues. Clinicians occupy the front row, center. When we come to work we implicitly accept this role. Many clinicians lose heart, somewhere along the way, and burn out. Often we can recognize when this happens to a colleague, who then plods through her last years of practice, going through the motions. I believe the burned out have failed to sustain the courage to face human dilemmas hour after hour.

Whether or not she treats patients as difficult as the Latin writer, where does any therapist get the courage she needs to function in her profession? How can the Latin writer's therapist bear the danger that the patient might take up permanent residence in hell, or try to enact his macabre sexual fantasies with her? What preparation can enable her to face possible expulsion from his world, at any point when his need for safe certainty outweighs his need for her? How can she face being loved by such a strange man, in such a strange relationship? What if he decides not to play by her rules? What if he refuses to sit, cooperate, use words, live in *her* world of reason? What if, instead, he tries to shock her, shake her up, get her to participate in his fantastic imaginings? What if he gets up from the chair and forces *his* rules on *her?*

She can't look too scared. She has to keep thinking. She has to keep finding her role, returning to it as to a home. But there are so many ways to get lost. How will she come close enough to understand this man, without frightening him or herself beyond what is bearable? How can she enter his hellish world of violence and sexual savagery and yet remain in her own world, guided by theory, reason, therapeutic intention? How can she let go enough to know him, but not so much that she loses herself?

This case provides a backdrop for studying courage, in treatment and other life situations. In the *Nicomachean Ethics,* Aristotle (fourth century B.C.) defines the virtue of courage as the observance of the mean between excessive fear and excessive rashness (p. 67). Then he says it is more complicated than this, however, for some things (like disgrace) should be feared. So, for Aristotle, the courageous person endures and fears the right things, for the right purpose, in the right manner, and at the right time. He feels and acts consistently with the present circumstances.

For Aristotle, it is even greater courage to be brave in response to sudden events because bravery "in unforeseen danger springs more from character, as there is less time for preparation; one might resolve to face a danger one can foresee, from calculation and on principle, but only a fixed disposition of courage will enable one to face sudden peril" (p. 71).

Two further pieces of advice from Aristotle (books two and three, pp. 31–82) seem to me to be especially relevant for the analyst:

1. Practice helps, that is, practice allows us to become braver by enduring fear-evoking situations.
2. If we are aware of our natural inclinations, we can compensate for them. If, for example, I know I tend to be overly fearful that a

patient will commit suicide, I can correct for this leaning. The wording of Aristotle's advice is amazingly apt for the analyst:

Notice what are the errors to which we are ourselves most prone (as different men are inclined by nature to different faults) and we shall discover what these are by observing the pleasure or pain that we experience; then we must drag ourselves away in the opposite direction, for by steering wide of our besetting error we shall make a middle course. This is the method adopted by carpenters to straighten warped timber [p. 46].

The analyst's courage is tested differently depending on the character issues presented by the patient. The ramifications of the match between the character of the analyst and that of the patient have been extensively explored by Kantrowitz (1996). In her research she studied analysts' self-reports of the personal impact of their work with patients. Interestingly her results concluded that areas of patient–analyst overlap are potential sources of mutual benefit, but they also pose the greatest challenges: "The situation is Janus-faced with pitfalls and opportunities" (p. 242). I have considered this issue elsewhere (Buechler, 2002c). Briefly, the patient's central character issues determine which aspect of the analyst's character is most salient to the treatment. Thus, with a schizoid patient, the analyst's intimacy issues, difficulties with intense emotion, and so on are most relevant. With an obsessional patient the analyst's tendencies to get into battles for control would be highlighted. For every character type, the optimal situation is for the analyst to experience personally the patient's central character issues to a moderate degree. This fosters the engagement of these issues in the transference–countertransference. For example, with an obsessional patient, the analyst has to have the capacity to be recruited into struggles over control, to experience them intensely enough with the patient. But if the analyst is too obsessional, he may not see how constricting the style is and what the patient sacrifices for it.

In the case that introduced this chapter, with a patient's escalating paranoid collapse, the analyst needs immense courage. The patient is experiencing an impending disaster that he may define in delusional terms, but he is in very real danger. His analyst must know her own "warps" well. She must be practiced in the courageous act of confronting unpredictable patients. She must be willing to bear risk, able to face the uncertain without forcing premature closure. She must respond "on the fly," without having foreseen the patient's imaginative leaps. She must neither succumb to fear nor deny it. In response to the patient's paranoid vulnerability, the analyst must find enough—but not too much—vulnerability of her own. As suggested earlier, I believe the optimal situation is for the patient's fundamental character issues to be reasonably familiar to the analyst personally, but not overwhelming. With the disturbed Latin writer, a courageous therapist is cognizant of all the work's considerable dangers, feels them intensely, and chooses to proceed.

In the presence of narcissistic character issues in the patient, the analyst must be moderately, but not overwhelmingly, narcissistically vulnerable so that he can risk injury to the patient's self-esteem and his own. To be too worried about this risk hamstrings the analyst. The everlastingly careful analyst, attempting to avoid narcissistically injuring the patient entirely misses opportunities for courageous interventions. On the other hand, the rash analyst may lose the patient through unnecessarily narcissistically injuring.

An example of the Aristotelian mean is the Fool's adroit handling of Lear in Shakespeare's play *King Lear*. At one point in the play (act I), there is little time left for Lear to face the truth about himself and, more generally, the human condition. Before the Fool's interventions, Lear is fixated on extravagant demonstrations of his importance. He must be central, in his daughters' lives and elsewhere. Initially the first two daughters are willing to fawn, but Cordelia is not. She and Kent are too blunt, too direct for Lear to tolerate. But the Fool gets his message across gradually. Early on he merely hints at the human challenges that await Lear ("Can you make no use of nothing, nuncle?"—that is, can you use your new poverty to teach you about the human condition?). During the storm (act III, scene 4, p. 108), Lear shows the deepened insight we would wish for ourselves and our patients when he says "take physic, pomp," and demands of himself

> Expose thyself to feel what wretches feel,
> That thou mayst shake the superflux to them,
> And show the heavens more just.

Can there be a more poignant expression of the journey from "pomp" to profound empathic understanding? Edmundson (2000) sums up Lear's transformation: "Before the play is over, Lear, tutored by the Fool, will show us how humane a vision can arise from losing all outward trappings, and seeing the essential fragility and preciousness of everything that lives" (p. 35).

In promoting Lear's awareness the Fool finds the Aristotelian mean between timidity and rashness. He is not so careful to preserve Lear's pride that he pulls his punches. Yet he leads Lear toward insight, rather than making pronouncements, as some other characters do. One remarkable example stands out. In act III (scene 6, p. 123), the Fool and Lear have a fascinating exchange. The Fool gives Lear a pithy interpretation ("He is mad that trusts in the tameness of a wolf, a horse's health, a boy's love, or a whore's oath"). At a time when Lear can hear it, the Fool points to Lear's fundamental misjudgment. He didn't expect each character to act according to her nature. Lear's response seems puzzling ("It shall be done; I will arraign them straight"). He has decided to hold a mock trial of his daughters. In other words, he has found a creative, imaginative expression for his rage. The Fool has subtly brought out how quintessentially human Lear's predicament is. In effect he says, "You have done what we are all sometimes tempted to do. You have made the mistake of expecting someone to act against their natural inclinations." Lear hears and then confines his towering rage to a civilized forum. He will imagine convicting his daughters, salve his pride, and then submit to a restorative sleep. I think as analysts we could hope for no better response!

The courage of the analyst faced with a narcissistic patient is expressed in a measured pursuit of the truth. It is not so timid as to reassure falsely, nor so rash as to prematurely confront. It takes only necessary risks of injury to the patient's sense of self, but takes these risks with a firm conviction that they are essential for the treatment, not retaliatory expressions of negative countertransference.

Faced with the patient's obsessionally indirect controlling behavior the analyst may manifest courage by using language boldly. For example, a patient talks about "having a difficult time" at work. She describes her boss's recent behavior, building a picture of the boss as irrational and harsh, but not naming these qualities. She talks about what she doesn't understand, repeating the phrase, "I don't get it." She reports being "upset" at work and tired at the end of the day, unsure how long she can "take it."

Although there are always many potential focuses in treatment, one possibility is to hear this language as obsessionally avoiding direct assertion. If the analyst's language sharply contrasts with the patient's, this can demonstrate the difference between the obsessional and nonobsessional use of words. Working this way takes courage, however, for it requires a bluntness that easily evokes anxiety in both participants. The analyst might ask, for example, "Why do you say you don't understand, when it is clear you really don't agree?" Or the analyst could comment, "You make your boss sound like an unreasonable tyrant." Both of these interventions highlight the patient's use of language; the first focuses on the patient's indirectness, the second emphasizes the patient's case building. Whenever we interpret obsessional language we run the risk of offending the patient, and the possibility of getting into an obsessional battle with him. Patients often respond defensively to these interpretations, insisting on the reasonableness of what they said. They may cling to logic or intellectualized arguments. The authority issue in the content may be played out in the process. That is, the patient's battle against adhering to the boss's procedures gives way to a battle against the analyst's interpretation.

Because a negative response to the confrontation of obsessional verbal defenses is so predictable, it may take courage for the analyst to make this interpretation. Of course, not every analyst will feel this confrontation is what is most desirable therapeutically. There is obviously room for differences of opinion about the role the analysis of a defense should play in any treatment. Where the issue of courage comes in is that it is essential that a variety of therapeutic moves should be available to the analyst, including the analysis of defense; this will only exist if the analyst has courage. With courage, the analyst could choose to confront obsessional defenses at any point.

Sullivan (1956) dressed this courage in sarcasm, announcing to an obsessional patient that her need to obscure their communication was about to lead to "the fog rolling in" (p. 245). I think the sarcastic cloak may undermine the effectiveness of the interpretation, substantiating the patient's feelings of being endangered. However we express ourselves, it sometimes takes real courage to call a spade a spade. To do so may require us to counter the patient's pressure and our own impulse to get through the hour with a minimum of exertion. It is work to confront obsessional indirectness. It is much easier simply to elicit more information, getting the patient to elaborate. But years can go by while we choose the safer course. We have probably all encountered patients who are veterans of long previous analyses that seem to have yielded relatively little. I often feel that a failure to counter and confront obsessional language bravely played a key role in such unfruitful analyses.

Patient and analyst can engage each other in stimulating discourse, with little change in how the patient actually lives life.

Tabling change can be part of a schizoid strategy for getting through life. The courage required of the analyst is the grit it takes to fight for "more life." With one of my patients, for example, a woman in her 40s in a highly successful career and a good marriage, I could easily simply get through each hour. Adept at all forms of coping, this patient filled sessions with engrossing stories about her life. I could slide through our time together exerting little effort, with muted emotions and expectations. In other words, the patient's "schizoid compromise" (Guntrip, 1969, pp. 288–310) can be contagious. Both patient and analyst can take the easy way out by manufacturing seeming conversation. At each session the patient can tell a vivid, evocative story about someone in her family, or at work, or a friend. I could respond with relatively predictable questions and reflections. Both of us could come through the 45 minutes feeling as though we had made human contact. We would have risked almost nothing and never been really surprised by what was said. The material could sound appropriate, sprinkled with enough genuine dilemma to look like the "stuff" of a treatment. Years could go by, stories could accumulate, we both could grow older with little really changing (in the treatment or in the rest of the patient's life).

The courage required of an analyst often lies halfway between rashness and timidity, as Aristotle suggested. An intervention could take the form of a prediction of the likely sequence of events ("If I react in the usual way to this story, we'll probably stay comfortable but go nowhere new today"). Timidity would dictate playing the "straight man." Rashness would jump to a brutal confrontation ("You are inviting me to waste time in meaningless pseudo-relating"). Courage, I would suggest, is finding a course midway between mindless repetitive enactment and harsh, blunt confrontation. The analyst's courage is shown in interventions that balance the need for tact with the need for truth, sacrificing neither. It takes courage to confront only if one is fully aware of the pain it may cause. It is easy to be brutally frank without empathy, and it is (relatively) easy to be empathic. What is difficult is finding a way to be empathic *and* frank. This requires conviction that avoiding wasting time and life is worth risking hurting people. It is not courageous to confront without empathy, for then too little is at stake for the analyst. She is merely an objective reporter describing the "facts," taking no risks. It is also not courageous to glide through time with a patient, seamlessly fulfilling the minimal expectations. Courage

is the determination to create a path in the uncharted territory in between these two extremes. It is finding a way to counter, rather than
join, schizoid compromises without any unnecessary injury to the
patient.

The Courage of Both Analytic Participants

She entered treatment in her mid-60s, divorced, with two grown children. Besides early losses of both parents, she had seen her ex-husband
die young. She had survived cancer and was weighing the risks versus
potential benefits of an elective surgery that might restore lost mobility. She counted many failures in her life—to develop a career after the
children grew up, to have a fulfilling marriage. Hers was a loveless and
essentially alienated relationship that officially ended long after any
real warmth had disappeared. For years she had tried to hang on to the
marriage despite its joylessness to give her children an intact family.

Now with no career, children geographically distant, friends disap-
pearing to illness and death, and increasingly compromised mobility,
she had one accomplishment to treasure. She had succeeded in raising
two wonderful children and had given them a good start in life. She
had endured her painful marriage until the children seemed old
enough to bear the breakup. She had many losses to look back on, but
at least she had been able to spare her children.

And then she got a letter from her son, accusing her of having
looked away from his father's sexually provocative behavior and impact. Sketchy but suggestive memories were coming up in this son's
therapy. He wanted her to rake up all she could recall to help him piece
together what had happened. Had his father ever really been sexually
inappropriate with the children?

For her, this was the last straw. Now even her self-image as a good,
protective mother was in jeopardy. Did she have to look at every family
photograph and comb her precious store of memories searching for
signs of sexual misconduct? Could it be true? Why hadn't she seen it?
Was she to lose everything, even her warm memories?

This patient's exploration of the past was as difficult as any journey
into the unknown can be. Barely suppressed anger made the journey
even harder.

While much was unclear to me in working with this patient, one
thing became obvious. Even if I tried to put my own values aside, they

would color my focus on the material. They would dictate what I thought of, noticed, asked about, overlooked, retained in memory. Selective curiosity is an implicit value judgment about what it is important to know (see chapter 1).

Was it right to help this patient dig up the past looking for "evidence"? What was it my responsibility to do? How did my own values about parenting, marriage, aging, facing the truth, and bearing loss affect my participation? I believe my values were most forcefully expressed in my actions, not my words. The patient could consider, agree, disagree, or ignore what I said. But she couldn't work with me exactly as she would have with another analyst whose values would shape her *focus* differently. What, in my heart, did I feel her son was entitled to? Did his mother have any right to limit the probing? Whose history, whose life is it anyway? Where should it stop? Was every family gathering, from here on, to become a judicial inquiry?

This patient was a woman of great courage. Her initial reaction to her son's demands may have been despairing, overwhelming grief and anger, but she didn't stop there. She faced her dilemma courageously. She would not err in either extreme, too timidly holding back or too rashly dashing forward. It was her courage that enabled her to meaningfully pursue the truth.

Although this was a somewhat unusual clinical situation, this patient's courage was far from unique. I do not measure my patient's courage (or my own) simply additively—that is, I don't assume the further we take an inquiry, the more courage we have shown. It isn't always more courageous to extend the process. Sometimes it shows more courage to define the *end* of an inquiry (for the moment, because it could always resume in the future). What I believe takes courage is assuming the responsibility to make judgment calls that are inevitably imperfect and bearing their consequences.

Patients and analysts show courage each time we confront demons, of whatever kind, with the strength to stare them down and the strength to let them be. Only when more than one alternative realistically exists, so a difficult assessment is required, can courage emerge. In the movie *Saving Private Ryan,* the commander shows courage not by blindly advancing into every line of fire, but bravely weighing consequences against each other, coming up with a judgment of which risk to take, and then bearing the responsibility for his decision. This is the courage required of the participants in an analysis, to face what it means to be human, every moment making choices we only partially understand. The courage of the patient isn't very different from that of the analyst. Both struggle with difficult judgment calls and both make their most courageous choices when the alternatives seem evenly matched and the stakes are high.

Aristotle as Supervisor

The two extremes Aristotle described are significant temptations in every analytic session. Succumbing to either rashness or timidity is always easier than bearing the tension between them. I believe that we can array analytic theoreticians according to which extreme they favored. This is, of course, oversimplification. Each analyst does more than merely position himself on the dimension of courage. But whatever else we do, it is inevitable that we take some stand on courage in how we conduct ourselves clinically, whether or not it is conscious.

Fromm and Sullivan, each in his own way, were willing, from my point of view, to err on the side of rashness. Sullivan's impatience and anger could, on occasion, push him to interpret punitively, not just bluntly. For example, Sullivan (1956, pp. 257–259) reports his clinical experience with a patient who was afraid of his own impulse to kill himself by flinging himself down a stairway. The patient clung to the ground floor in the hospital, to avoid this impulse. Sullivan, feeling frustrated at their lack of progress, told the patient "I am transferring you to the second floor now, and issuing orders that you will not be served a tray. And so, I don't know; maybe you will die by flinging yourself over the stairs; I doubt it. Maybe you will starve to death; I doubt that too. But we'll have to see" (p. 259).

Sullivan admits he would not cite this case as an instance of particularly good treatment, but he was advocating putting pressure on the patient to give up the symptoms. Surely he was taking a serious risk. Sullivan could have goaded the patient into acting on the self-destructive impulse. We might see Sullivan as rash in his handling of this situation. I believe in this instance frustration pushed Sullivan toward cruelty in his manner of expression, although the clinical judgment in favor of confronting the symptom may have been sound.

Sullivan's avowed goal, which was, at times, to get the treatment moving (e.g., 1956, p. 371), can bring him to the brink of a dangerous rashness. Take, for example, the case (1956, pp. 376–378) "selected as summing up Sullivan's overall approach to both schizophrenia and mental disorder in general, since it seems to synthesize much of his attitude toward patients in terms of both theoretic and human considerations" (pp. 376–377). The patient is a young schizophrenic boy who has had a disastrous love affair that he is trying to pass off as insignificant. Sullivan's advice to the clinician is this: "If the psychiatrist swiftly comes back with something like "Nonsense, you were happy with her," he may have opened the patient's mind. It is the very speed and directness of a completely unsuspected comment like that which sometimes fixes vividly the involuntary attention of the patient" (p. 377).

Sullivan's advice continues, "In a situation of this kind, once I have startled the patient into any alertness by some variant of 'Nonsense, you liked her,' I continue the attack" (p. 377).

I think there can be no question that Sullivan had profound empathy for this severely disturbed patient and was trying (desperately) to get through to him. But I would say that desperation can, on occasion, lead to rashness. Even Sullivan's language ("startled," "attack") suggests his determined use of force to penetrate this patient's defenses. This is especially striking in that Sullivan was working in an era when the rule of thumb was to break through the defenses of the neurotic patient, and *support* the defenses of the more severely disturbed (Knight, 1953).

I am convinced Sullivan was trying to push the patient into life, like slapping a newborn infant into breathing. It takes courage. But it depends on adroit risk taking and delicate judgment calls. What if it goes too far, too fast?

Fromm, too, could err on the side of rashness. Maccoby (1996), who was in treatment with Fromm and collaborated with him on a book (*Social Character in a Mexican Village;* Fromm and Maccoby, 1970), identified two voices in Fromm: the prophetic and the analytic. Maccoby writes of how sometimes the prophet in Fromm eclipsed the analyst:

> Fromm believed that the psychoanalyst should be active and penetrating, bringing the session to life by demonstrating his own urgency to understand and grasp life fully. Here the prophetic voice sometimes overwhelmed analysis. Fromm became like a religious master who unmasks illusions and thus expands the limits of the social filter, dissolving resistances. By experiencing and confessing to one's unconscious im-

pulses, the patient would gain the energy and strength to change his or her life, and to develop human capabilities for love and reason to the fullest. This is an unproven theory, and in practice Fromm's technique sometimes resulted in a very different outcome [p. 75].

Fromm has been, rightly I believe, praised for his courage as a theoretician (Roazen, 1996). He challenged the status quo in the analytic community and in the wider society (Funk, 1982; Burston, 1991; Cortina and Maccoby, 1996). In the consulting room, however, this passionate advocacy for healthy living could translate into pressure on the patient, giving short shrift to analytic exploration. The analyst's urgent need for a preordained outcome can be manifested in an exhorting style. The prophetic analyst sometimes interprets rashly, in too big a hurry to bring the patient to the desired outcome.

Burston (1991) notes the irony that Fromm, whose intention was to redress conformist abuses, compelled as much submission to his own authority as any classical analyst. In Burston's view, "having formulated a patient's 'core' problem to his own satisfaction, he would often adopt a didactic, prescriptive stance and interpret conflicting testimony, no matter how compelling, as 'resistance'" (p. 82).

What Freud's imposing oedipal meanings, Sullivan's insisting on more adaptive behaviors, and Fromm's preaching about psychological health have in common is this rashness. They are all so convinced they know where they want to go with the patient that they can't wait to get there. Treatment becomes a headlong dash. The patient is put in the position of having to choose between a compliance that can feel like self-betrayal versus defiance of the analyst. In this context, the patient is unlikely to find his own truth.

Fromm was, I believe, trying to save time and pull the patient quickly toward health. In his own words,

I would suggest we consider that among the light forms of neurosis many might be cured but by methods much shorter than two years of analysis, that is to say, by having the courage of using analytic insight to approach the patient very directly, to approach the problem very directly, and possibly to do in 20 hours what one feels obligated to do, as an analyst, in 200 hours. There is no reason for false shame to use direct methods when they can be used [Fromm, 1964a, pp. 601–602].

Here Fromm defines analytic courage in a way that I would see as rashness, an extreme that diverges from the truly courageous. We can see the dangers of rashness in Fromm's paper, which describes a rare example of clinical treatment conducted and discussed by him (pp. 581–602). Fromm celebrates the patient's development from a homosexual liaison to "a perfectly normal girl, with normal reactions" (p. 589). Fromm believes this frightened girl found her true self in the treatment, but the reader can be left with an uneasy impression that the patient may have merely complied with the analyst's personal notions of psychological health, consciously or unconsciously.

It is not necessarily courageous to enact Freud's urgency to adapt Dora, or Sullivan's need to get his patient to climb the staircase, or Fromm's zeal to get his patient to commit to a lifestyle. The courageous analyst feels these pulls and the press of time—the urgency about not wasting life—but also feels an equal pull against imposing his values on the patient. Courage involves awareness of all the dangers, not just one set. With courage we know how very many ways we can fail—by rashly indoctrinating, coercing the patient to comply with our own personal vision of health; or by timidly clinging to an arid neutrality. Courage is acting despite knowing that the quality of a life is at stake, and we can err without realizing it if we move too quickly or too slowly. To keep moving forward under those conditions takes real courage.

To the extent that the analyst narrows his vision of his role so that he doesn't have to have the courage to acknowledge the impact of his own values about life on the treatment, he errs in the timid direction. Analysts have historically looked for an acceptable way to define our role. We have cultivated the image of the classically neutral Freudian "surgeon" (Freud, 1912), the Kleinian repository for projections (Klein, 1961), the passive reflecting facilitator (Rogers, 1961), the Winnicottian container (Winnicott, 1965), the Levensonian demystifier (Levenson, 1991), and the postmodern dialectical-constructivist (Hoffman, 1998). Each of these can be seen as an attempt to describe our role and our impact on treatment's goals. Each description locates the author on the dimension of courage. This is not meant pejoratively. It does not apply to these authors more than any other. In fact, we could take any description of our role, or any clinical moment, and locate it somewhere on a continuum from rash to timid. How much are we facilitating a patient-directed journey through life versus how much do we actually participate in defining the patient's destination (Mitchell, 1997)? Perhaps our greatest challenge in analysis is finding a way to avoid the extreme of rash indoctrination into what we personally see as health but also to avoid the extreme of excessive timidity about our impact. To be capable of avoiding both of these extremes the courageous analyst has to bear full responsibility for choosing how to use her very real influence on the patient's vision of life.

Courage in the analyst can be understood as the ability to consciously risk doing harm, or, more often, to risk failing to help. Only the analyst who can bear regret, guilt, and shame can plunge ahead knowing what is at stake. The more we grasp the complexity of our task, the more courage it takes to keep making close judgment calls. What should be confronted, when, and how? What should be heard and, for the moment, left alone? To be analysts, we have to have confidence that we can live with ourselves, regardless of the outcome of our judgments.

I believe that clinical courage depends on comfort with one's own superego. For example, to have real choices with my patient (whose son suspected paternal sexual inappropriateness), I would have to have a loving enough superego (Schecter, 1979) to be able to risk doing harm. If I were merely to have delineated her choices, I would have done nothing that could come back to haunt me. But if I "vote" for inquiry into her son's charges, I risk angering the patient or failing to support her fragile healthy entitlement. "Voting" against inquiry would take different risks (that her son could claim she failed him, and she could come to agree). I have no problem seeing it as legitimate that another clinician could argue for a different position from my own. What I do believe is that to have all the options available, we need the courage that only our own loving, forgiving superego can engender. Bolstered by this inner ballast, we can manifest courage. The process can match the content, in that both express forthrightness (see also chapter 8 on integrity).

From an emotion theory point of view, clinical courage requires the capacity to bear shame, guilt, surprise, anxiety, and, probably, loneliness. As defined by Fromm-Reichmann (1959) loneliness implies an absence of the expectation of human connection. The clinician must be prepared to bear being alone with her point of view for the foreseeable future.

This strikes me as similar in spirit to Zeddies's (2002, p. 429) description of

> helping patients to face and integrate into self-awareness the alien, rejected, repressed, unformulated, unfamiliar, unvalidated, or otherwise unknown aspects of themselves. What is needed much of the time is an increased comfort with—or at least the courage not to flee from—the unknown in ourselves, our patients, and the analytic setting more generally (Eisold, 2000; Zeddies, 2000c). Being comfortable *enough* with the unknown pertains to the capacity to experience uncertainty and surprise.

Thus, courage is the quality, perhaps more than any other, that has been increasingly called for ever since analytic thinking lost the certainties of the classical model. No matter how theory evolves in this post-postmodern era, I don't believe we will ever again match Freud's conviction about the efficacy of insight, and the oedipal derivation of neurosis. It is inevitable that awareness of our subjectivity highlights the necessity for courage. Of course, in his day Freud and other psychoanalytic pioneers needed enormous courage too, fighting their own lone battles. But in our era we must courageously bear the heavy responsibility of making constant judgment calls, without an a priori, universally accepted conception of mental health, pathology, treatment's objectives, therapeutic action, and so on.

D. Stern and his associates (1998) provide another language for clinical courage when they write about facing disruption, or "now moments." Altman (2002, p. 503) puts this succinctly when he says

> These moments feel, subjectively, like crises in which the relationship itself is at risk. Both therapist and patient feel naked, without defenses. If both parties can find a way to act authentically and spontaneously, the old procedural patterning of their interaction can open up: change can occur in structured procedural knowledge. In other words, change can occur in presymbolic relational patterning, working models of human interaction, the internal world. The content of verbalization per se is not key in this model of the therapeutic process; authenticity and the willingness to take risks are more important.

Earlier Altman (2002, pp. 501–502) cites a clinical vignette that I think beautifully illustrates the courageous clinical judgment call. In this vignette the patient has had brain surgery away from her hometown and will need a piece of her skull reinserted. On the day of her session, the patient has learned this precious body part was in transit to her local doctor—in the ordinary mail! Her analyst (A. Alvarez, who wrote about this case in the 1992 book, *Live Company*) has to walk a tightrope between overreacting and underreacting to the situation. The analyst's stated goal is for the patient to own her own anxiety and not shift it to the analyst (which might be induced if the analyst overreacts) or distance from it (which could be prompted by the analyst's underreaction).

In discussing the therapeutic action in this situation Altman emphasized the analyst's poetic language and affective intensity. An important element is the courage Alvarez had to face the fact that she might be overreacting or that her emotionality could make her appear foolish or overanxious. It is living this courage in front of the patient that I believe probably had the greatest therapeutic impact. When we face "now moments" authentically and forthrightly, this action often has a more powerful message than the content of what we say. Thus, for me, the meaning of the "now moment" is that it gives the analyst an opportunity to manifest courage palpably. The weight of our responsibility includes knowing we leave our personal mark on every patient we see (Ehrenberg, 1992; Maroda, 2002). We can never be sure our impact was the best possible influence we could have had on the patient's life. We must live with being human and fallible yet are required to choose which side to take in complicated judgment calls. Should the patient's defenses be bolstered rather than analyzed at this point? Despite having no clairvoyance about dangers that may exist, we have to make continual choices.

Historically we have found many ways to describe our perilous task, but whatever terms we choose, we have to realize that it doesn't take any more courage to provoke than it does to interpret neutrally, reflect, facilitate, or hold. What takes great courage is to be fully human, fallible, and yet responsible for the impact of our choices. We are not less responsible because our judgment calls are difficult.

An analyst who lives each session courageously, sometimes naming the dangers but still struggling forward, promotes courage in the patient. I had to tell the patient I mentioned earlier (whose son demanded revisiting family memories looking for possible sexual abuse) that I was afraid I might uphold the value of searching for the truth, out of my own personal needs. But, I told her, I also had the impulse to support the patient's newly budding sense of entitlement to do what she felt was best for her, rather than sacrifice herself for others. First I had to make these value judgments a mutual problem rather than assume I could rely on a technique to "purify" my actions of the taint of my personal beliefs about life. Every move on the part of the analyst, every detail attended to or unattended is a judgment of priorities about life.

Naming the issues is not enough to promote courage in the patient— it is necessary but not sufficient. I also had to embrace one set of dangers more than others to promote active courage. I had to take a clear position so that the patient could find her own stance by comparing and contrasting it with mine. I had to live out loud for her. This took being willing to be proven wrong, foolish, and harmful. While accepting that my judgment call (in this case, in favor of the search) reflected only *a* way to live life, that is, *my* way to live life, and not *the* way to live, I still had to voice it. I don't know the way to be human, but when I can give voice to *my* way and take responsibility for its influence, I am promoting courage more powerfully than if I either timidly waited or rashly promoted a position without any self-reflection on what was at stake for me. My actions, and not just my words, are communicating the value of moving forward, despite an awareness of imperfection. By naming the human dilemmas, as I see them in the material, and then taking a position, I manifest my belief that doing some harm is the unfortunate, inevitable, but bearable price of being human.

Essential Equipment

What enables the analyst to have sufficient courage to occupy such a lonely outpost, with such meager and uncertain provisions for his own self-esteem? What can fortify him enough to avoid the temptation of flashy rashness and the equally alluring temptation of safe timidity? In short, how do we inculcate Aristotelian courage in the analyst?

It is, first of all, in training that we need to begin to equip the analyst to have courage (Buechler, 1997). Analysts, in my experience, have a peculiar reluctance to talk with candidates (or with each other) about the personal qualities our work requires. Yet we all know that on every level, physical as well as psychological, it is a feat of stamina to concentrate intensely on patients for a long workday. Training should begin the candidate's development of

1. Awareness of the sheer physical difficulty of an analyst's life.
2. Empathy for the heavy moral, ethical, psychological, intellectual, and affective burdens of an analyst (Buechler, 1998, 2000).
3. A supportive relationship with one's own superego, providing ready access to the sense of being worthwhile, well-intentioned, and so on, which I have referred to elsewhere (Buechler, 1998) as the analyst's "internal chorus."
4. Forgiveness, that is, reasonable levels of shame, anxiety, guilt, and regret for mistakes.
5. Ongoing identity, despite being the repository of projective identifications.

The internally well-equipped analyst can show courage because she doesn't need a success with this patient to prove herself. She has already proven herself (Buechler, 1999). She doesn't need a self-congratulatory ego boost from rash, showy moves (like Sullivan's taunt to the patient who was afraid he would jump from the second floor). She also doesn't need the self-comfort a timid stance can buy. Had I, for example, merely reflected my patient's difficult choice with her son I could have told myself I was only following (analytic) orders, supplying a needed neutral mirror.

Of course a reasoned therapeutic interpretation to one analyst may seem rash to another, and one analyst's timidity may be another's good judgment. Our perspectives are inherently, eternally subjective. It is not any particular behavior that confirms the analyst's courage. Analytic courage establishes a palpable atmosphere of profound freedom of speech. It is the *feeling* of being with the child who, at any moment, might say the emperor had no clothes on. In this child's company anything can happen next. No thought is taboo; and anything that can be thought may be spoken. But this child wouldn't lose her sense of being herself if she chose *not* to point out the emperor's nakedness. In her presence, there is always the possibility, but not the certainty, that the previously unspoken will be given voice.

5   *Manifesting a Sense of Purpose*

We tend not to speak or write much of the analyst's hopes as
such, because that sounds too personal somehow. The analyst
is portrayed as a professional, providing a generic service that
helps when applied properly. But we all know that it is much
more personal than that, that the analyst's hopes for her patients are embedded in and deeply entangled with her own
sense of self, her worth, what she can offer, what she has found
deeply meaningful in her own life. The more we have explored
the complexities of countertransference, the more we have
come to realize how personal a stake the analyst inevitably has
in the proceedings. It is important to be able to help; it makes us
anxious when we are prevented from helping or do not know
how to help. Our hopes for the patient are inextricably bound
up with our hopes for ourselves.

              —Stephen Mitchell, *Hope and Dread in Psychoanalysis*

With his usual clarity and candor Mitchell has made an essential point. Our hopes (or goals, or purposes) as analysts are personal. Yet I argue that both analytic participants need a *sense of purpose,*

Dr. Mark Blechner contributed greatly to the evolution of this chapter.

a quality, similar to curiosity, hope, courage, emotional balance, the ability to bear loss, and integrity, that the analyst must manifest in the texture of her work. I suggest that valuing this sense of purpose (vs. valuing only *specific* goals) is part of our analytic culture (Zeddies, 2002). This chapter explores the sense of purpose as a treatment necessity, for analyst and for patient.

Sullivan (1954, p. 4) stated that the patient must "expect to derive benefit" from the session. Although true, this leaves out what the *analyst* expects, for the patient and for herself. Each of us has a personal rendition of our hopes for our work, and even this personal rendition probably varies to some degree with different patients, but the need for a sense of purpose cuts across all analysts and all patients.

I believe that the ideal of neutrality (A. Freud, 1936; Poland, 1984; Jacobs, 1986; Abend, 1989) may have hindered our clarification of our stake in the work. It interfered with identifying our specific personal needs and the professional culture's values. Holding the ideal of neutrality made it hard for us to communicate with each other about our other ideals and sometimes even to recognize them ourselves.

Previously (Buechler, 1999, 2002b) I have described what I feel was problematic about the ideal of neutrality. Briefly, it did not, among its other limitations, allow enough room for the expression of countertransferential passions. In a 1999 paper on searching for a passionate neutrality I explored how we might balance some of the benefits of the classical role with some of the benefits of greater expressivity of our subjective affects. I discussed how this might be particularly useful in the work with severely depressed patients, who may especially need help to actively fight the depressive pull. What I suggest in this chapter may be seen as an extension of this view about neutrality. The ideal of neutrality made it difficult to face yearnings we bring to our work, to express them with patients and with each other, and to confront the value the profession places on having a sense of purpose.

The ideal of neutrality has not been our only obstacle, however. It has been enticing, at least for some of us, to see ourselves as working solely to meet the needs of others. The neutral "surgeon," impassively toiling to remove "pathology," served as a heroic image.

I would like to identify what I see as the components of the analyst's sense of purpose. This overall "sense" or attitude of purposefulness can be differentiated from the specific goals of any particular treatment.

Briefly, purposefulness in treatment includes, I believe, the expectation of movement and meaningfulness, and a paradoxical relationship to time. That is, an attitude of purposefulness is expressed in an analytic focus that moves, looks for meaning, and both embraces and eradicates time. To have a sense of purpose, clinical work has to exist within a specific time in the participants' lives, but also *outside* that time. I explore and clinically illustrate each of these components of the sense of purpose in the remainder of this chapter.

The Analyst's Restless Focus

For both participants a sense of purpose includes an expectation of movement, but I am concentrating on how this is experienced and expressed by the analyst. We are accustomed to patients' importunate cries that treatment is taking too long; that they need to feel better now and not invest endless time and money in the process without tangible immediate results. Elsewhere (Buechler, 1999) I have suggested that patients' investment in improving the quality of their current lives is a vital motivating force that should be cultivated. I don't agree with the attitude I sometimes encounter that patients who want fast results have to learn to delay gratification. Although this certainly can be a necessity at times, I feel it is equally important to cherish this "impatience" in patients. They *should* want a good life now, as well as in the future. We all do.

I wish to concentrate on the analyst's urge toward movement, however, because I believe it is expressed in her focus, minute by minute, in the session. In a less microscopic sense, I believe our yearning for movement is often achingly clear at clinical presentations. An uneasy, contradictory attitude can prevail, particularly when candidates describe their clinical work. They are, I feel, given the mixed message that what "counts" is the analytic quality of the treatment, that is, whether the process reflects proper emphasis on the transference and the analysis of defense. Yet everyone is often quite evidently relieved when there are also tangible positive results now. We all (including, of course, the candidate) feel better if the patient is less suicidal, less symptomatic than he was at the outset of treatment. We espouse adherence to valuing long-term change over short-term symptom relief, but we are much more comfortable when we can see palpable evidence of both. In what I often experience as a comically convoluted performance, candidates casually mention the concrete results while seemingly concentrating on the analytic process. In a kind of "dumb show," they reassure us by indicating both the patient's symptom relief and their own "proper" analytic emphasis. Thus they lead us to notice the patient feels better, without themselves seeming too caught up in "therapeutic zeal."

But I suggest it is in our minute-to-minute focus in a session that we manifest our own need for movement most clearly. Treating children indelibly impressed me with the human striving toward what is next. I remember the four-year-old scoffing at his three-year-old sister, contemptuously labeling her a "baby." I think we all have within us the child who wanted to walk as soon as she crawled.

I am very aware of this urge in myself, both in and outside my clinical work. Let me hasten to add that I know contrary impulses can also prevail. For me, however, working clinically often calls out a purposeful forward motion.

This push is not spoken of directly (most of the time), but it is manifested in many ways. The most frequent manifestation of the need for movement is, I believe, the absence of an expression of interest. For example, when I don't pick up on something the patient says, I am, through that inaction, expressing an absence of interest in staying where we are and exploring it further. I am not saying directly, "Let's move on," and I may not even consciously have that thought, but I am manifesting a willingness to move on.

I believe we express the propensity for movement most often in our focus or lack of focus. There are, of course, countless verbal and nonverbal cues that we could pick up on. Silence about any one of them says, in effect, "It is fine with me not to stay with this." On the other hand, through questions, interpretations, empathic reflections, repetitions, and rewordings, we say "stay," at least for the moment.

The urge forward is more directly expressed in various forms of restlessness. Some are more overt—some are verbal, some nonverbal. Just as I interpret the patient's foot tapping, she may interpret my restless gaze.

Rhythmic expressions of restlessness are also frequent. If I hardly pause after the patient speaks, I am, in my pace alone, manifesting the urge to move on.

Let me emphasize that I am not suggesting we define for patients what "movement forward" in their lives would look like. I am not referring to being directive about a "right" or "progressive" way to live. I am saying, however, that we manifest the urge forward in our focus on the material, in the absence of response, in verbal and nonverbal signs of restlessness, and in the rhythms of our speech.

In all these ways, we manifest an unwillingness to stay forever still, or an expectation of movement. This expectation is key to conveying a sense of purpose. By "telling" patients, mainly through how we focus on the material, that we expect movement, we communicate a value that, I believe, we ourselves imbibed during our training. Of course our professional training occurs long after our initial "training" to be human beings. We each bring a personal style to our training in analytic focusing. I had a personal expectation of movement that was part of my sense of purpose long before I was trained analytically. But, along with Zeddies (2002), I believe our professional culture imbues us with a set of values. The personal and the professional values we hold are likely to overlap and reinforce each other. I cannot say how much my clinical purposes stem from my personal history, my particular training experiences, the professional culture, and so on. By definition, I am unable to be objective about this. I believe, however, that growing up professionally in a psychoanalytic climate breeds commonalities, although, of course, each theoretical belief system creates differences as well (see chapter 9).

In my own case, personal "purposefulness," including an expectation of movement, is a core part of my personality, and I am sure it influenced my choice of profession. Looking back, I think it also played a role in who I chose as my analyst and my supervisors. But then they, and the professional culture as a whole, had an impact on my values. My own "expectation of movement" was especially reinforced by early professional experience working in hospitals with psychotic adults and working in various settings with children. In both of these settings, it is a common experience to need to get somewhere. My personal urge forward was enhanced by wanting to help psychiatric patients "move" to more normal lives and wanting to help children grow. In choosing to work in these settings, I expressed who I already was, but, I am sure, these experiences also shaped me. I brought all of this to my analytic training, which profoundly reinforced the need to have and to convey a sense of purpose. An "atmosphere" of purposefulness was certainly part of the air I breathed in my personal analysis. I will never be able to separate the role of my personal experience and character development from my early professional work and later analytic training in forming the analyst I have become. But I feel certain that all of these experiences contributed to my strong conviction that a sense of movement and purpose is a vital ingredient for both treatment participants.

Making Meaning

Creating meaning through the interpretive act is clearly too vast a topic to address here. I offer some reflections on how the making of meaning plays a role in my own clinical effort to manifest a sense of purpose.

My belief is that the manifestation of a sense of purpose is vital to every treatment, but it is especially important in the work with patients who, themselves, have not been able to find meaningful purpose. Although a hallmark of narcissism (Fiscalini, 1995), the difficulty creating a meaningful life, with a sense of purpose, transcends any "group."

In the astute short story "The Dilettante," Thomas Mann (1961) gives us a memoir of a man who never finds purpose. Like many patients, the man is attractive and promising when young but, with age, increasingly uncertain what to do with his life and increasingly anxious to be sure he will turn out a winner. He becomes more and more desperate to be praised and happy, for only then could he count his life a success. And without demonstrable success life has no purpose for him. Predictably, by the end of the memoir he has lost all hope: "Yes, I am unhappy: I freely admit it, I seem a lamentable and absurd figure even to myself. And that I cannot bear. I shall make an end of it. Today, or tomorrow, or some time, I will shoot myself. . . . what is destroying me is that hope has been destroyed with the destruction of all pleasure in myself" (p. 59).

Why is it that some people seem able to find purpose and others aimlessly drift through life? It is as though in the process of composing the story of their lives they developed writer's block. With age the search for purpose takes on a desperate, flailing quality. They cannot complete the story of their own lives because they run out of plot. Stories generally go somewhere. Theirs have no direction. Yet, like Mann's dilettante they may have had early promise. When young they seemed well equipped for life. By middle age it becomes clear that something is missing. They are unable to reliably find meaning in their lives.

One patient, a middle-aged secondary-school teacher, contemplates retirement with anxiety. Routine has made living possible. But without the need to rise at a certain time, how will he ever get up? Without a mandatory schedule, how will he invent each day? He drifted into teaching and moored there for 30 years. He is clearly a talented teacher, although he hates society's blatant disregard for the profession, but he gets minimal personal gratification, self-esteem, or self-definition from his work. The praise he earns keeps him getting up in the morning—barely. He is like someone on a severe diet: he gets just enough for minimal functioning. Raise the level of energy his life requires or lower the praise intake, and he wouldn't be able to keep moving at all. Praise gives his life meaning.

As Thomas Mann's dilettante discovered this is a deadly bargain. When the praise runs out, motivation is gone. It reminds me of a windup toy, getting its "fix" and sailing along for a while, then sputtering to a complete stop. But how does anyone find the kind of inner driving purpose that can function independent of praise? The Van Goghs, Mozarts, and Dostoevskys of this world go on creating, year after year, with or without acclaim. Perhaps they derive a sense of meaningful purpose from their awareness of having great talent. But what about the rest of us?

I ask another patient, a highly successful professional in middle age, what he likes to do in his (limited) spare time. There is a long silence. He is dumbfounded. He has no idea what he likes to do. The question has never occurred to him. It is extremely unsettling for him to realize this.

A younger patient keeps endlessly busy, sometimes aware of avoiding unfilled time. Unoccupied, how would she keep from a depressive collapse? Without self-defining activity, who would she be?

I believe that, especially with these patients, but with every patient, it is essential to the work that I convey the following:

1. For me there is inherent meaning in the patient's life, and therefore I feel a sense of purpose in working to improve the quality of that life.
2. I am willing to fight for the life of the treatment, because it is meaningful to me.
3. The treatment's overall health is more meaningful than my pride, if I have to choose between them.
4. Meaningful self-reflection is something to be proud of, regardless of what it reveals.
5. I am not ashamed of my intensity of purpose. Passionately wanting the patient to find a meaningful life is not a source of conflict for me.

In how we live the session, we convey what we find meaningful and what gives us a sense of purpose. Much of this is expressed in our tone, rather than in our choice of words. Tone can manifest passion about the work. I have often experienced treatment as a kind of fight for life. I think this fighting spirit pervades the writing of Erich Fromm (1941, 1947, 1964b, 1973).

Greenberg (1991) cautions us that if we present too much of a new and affirmative "object" to the patient, we may inhibit the expression of the patient's self-destructive urges. This is a significant danger. It is equally important to convey passionate purpose, however. Both aims can be accomplished, in that our words can express an invitation for the patient to voice her whole self, including self-destructive impulses. But our tone, tempo, and passionate purpose can still be felt. Words and tone can have different jobs.

In how we treat ourselves, as "objects," we live our values in front of the patient. We show what really matters to us. That is, in front of the patient, we must cope with our own narcissistic needs without allowing them to dominate us. We must value life over image. Sometimes we must be willing to look like fools.

On the most concrete level, this is played out in the clinician's handling of potentially shame-inducing moments in the treatment. How do I react to my own mistakes? What do I do with my own slips of the tongue? When the patient accuses me of not helping, questions the value of our work, or, more generally, the value of treatment, do I respond defensively? Must I uphold my own image, at all costs? Must I look smart, right, well intentioned, intuitive, emotionally responsive, self-contained? Must I emerge from every conflictual interchange "smelling like a rose"? Am I willing to take interpersonal risks in the name of the treatment? Will I say what can sound foolish if I think it is right, and risk the patient's scorn, dismissal, contempt?

On a more subtle level, how much do I need credit for the treatment's accomplishments? More generally, do I take credit for the *patient's* accomplishments?

How easily can I allow myself to cry in front of the patient or ask potentially foolish-sounding questions? Can I be "childishly" eager, openly curious? Can I need help? In areas in which the patient is more expert, can I ask for information? What is the *feel* of moments when I'm the one who asks, or needs, or is more emotional?

It often seems to me, when clinicians credit self-disclosure as having helped a patient (Maroda, 1999) that what helped wasn't the disclosure itself, but the values embodied in the act of disclosing. The analyst is saying, "I'm willing to give you information that you could use to shame me. I'm willing to do whatever it takes to reach you." He is embodying the idea that the treatment comes before his pride, and, more generally, that life is more important than image. I view the "therapeutic action" of the work on empathic failures similarly. What I believe the patient derives from this work has mainly to do with how the analyst relates to his own self-esteem. As analyst and patient explore an empathic failure in the treatment, how does the analyst treat himself? Is he harshly self-critical, or can he comfortably hold himself responsible for his actions without becoming self-punitive? Can he take some real responsibility for his own negative impact, however consciously well intended it might have been? I see the impact of the work on empathic failures as deriving mainly from their providing an opportunity for the clinician to fail, react without undue shame, guilt, or denial, and move on. We have a vast array of opportunities to manifest a sense of purpose. When a session time must be changed, what do we convey about the importance of finding an alternative? What does the analyst convey about the importance of the treatment to her? Does she think about the work, even when she doesn't have to? Does she (obviously) work hard? How much emotional investment is the treatment (and, by extension, life itself) worth to her? If the patient begins to lose motivation, how hard does the analyst fight for the treatment? Will she take a stand, for example, about the need to maintain the frequency of sessions? Is she willing to fight for the treatment to have a full life, rather than be prematurely terminated?

Treatment is inherently shame inducing (Buechler, 1993) because it requires the patient to face all of himself. We must embody the attitude that no matter what the patient sees when he looks in the mirror, he deserves credit for looking—the courageous integrity it takes to be a patient must be seen by both patient and analyst. In a departure, perhaps, from the patient's earlier experience, in the treatment the patient must feel respected for the act of self-confrontation, even though some of what is confronted may evoke shame. This "credit" may enable the patient to keep digging, to value the pursuit of self-knowledge over the pursuit of all-positive self-reflections. Instead of needing to feel good because, in each session, he looks good to himself, he will become able to feel good because he looks *at* himself. Many patients enter treatment unable to extend themselves this credit. In every possible way, we must manifest the inherent value of insight, treatment, and, more generally, the fully explored life.

Thus the analyst relationally challenges the patient in how he lives the session. By caring about the work for itself, not for how it makes us look, we embody a different way of living in the world. Manifesting these values is, in itself, a kind of interpretation—and a vital aspect of the work.

By being openly self-reflective about our shortcomings and limitations, we offer ourselves as a catalyst for whatever in the patient can honestly self-reflect. One person looking in the mirror without shame encourages another to do the same. Most important, I think, is the relational challenge we pose. We must make it hard for the patient to continue to see life as having no purpose. Our own passionate purposefulness must make his cynicism difficult to maintain. Through what we manifest, we issue a challenge. We *show* that life is inherently important and that there is much of value to accomplish.

In Time and Outside Time

In the spirit of Hoffman (1998), I am fascinated by the paradoxical nature of our work. We are neutral caregivers who express genuine feeling, provided we are paid for it. Hoffman has eloquently drawn the analogy to prostitution.

Our work leaves much room for playful witticism. No area seems to me more paradoxical than the analyst's relationship to time. Although many aspects of this relationship would be interesting to address, I consider only the paradoxical nature of how we locate the treatment in time. Briefly, I suggest that it is integral to manifesting our sense of purpose that we locate ourselves within a time frame and also outside time. That is, I feel it essential to clarify *when* the treatment is occurring, in the chronology of the participants' lives. But it is just as essential that the work exist outside time, at no particular time in our lives. Freedom from time's constraints is part of the work's joy, for both participants.

Making Time

My last sentence is to say that I would suggest we consider that among the light forms of neurosis many might be cured but by methods much shorter than two years of analysis, that is to say, by having the courage of using analytic insight to approach the patient very directly, to approach the problem very directly, and possibly to do in 20 hours what one feels obligated to do, as an analyst, in 200 hours. There is no reason for false shame to use direct methods when they can be used [Fromm, 1964a, pp. 601–602].

A profound awareness of time, and an appreciation of its preciousness, is part of our legacy from Fromm. Although perhaps sometimes in too much of a hurry (Maccoby, 1996), Fromm, in a positive sense, advocated regard for the meaningfulness of time (and, by extension, of life itself). He was impatient with the wasting of time. This attitude can give the analyst "fire in her belly." It imbues every session with a strong sense of purpose. We have work to do and limited time in which to do it.

Respect for time is analytically expressed in many ways. When we don't let much time go by without sharpening our vision of the treatment's goals, we are manifesting concern about time. When we show care to clarify the patient's history, or any chronology of events, our actions are expressing the belief that the time frame counts, sequence matters, and the duration of an experience can make a difference.

Whenever patients tell us a dream and we ask when they had it, we are implying that knowing when the dream happened may help us make use of the dream. More generally, when we use an event's location in time to understand the meaning of the event, we are suggesting that timing matters.

We manifest a relationship to time by treating it as important, in many ways. It counts, to us, as a central aspect of the frame. Timing of interpretations has always been a crucial aspect of technique. Spacing of sessions, so there is some time between them for reflection, but not so much time that the thread is lost, is important to the work. When time is lost (because of lateness or missed sessions), I believe this should be treated as significant. I usually speak of an interruption in the rhythm of the work and look for its impact.

I am manifesting my respect for time and a kind of willingness to live within its boundaries. It is, to me, an acceptance of the terms of life. It allows experiences to be more clearly defined. I think it offers a meaningful contrast with, most especially, the narcissistic unwillingness to accept the limitations of being a human being. In the mind of the person who is prevailingly narcissistic, human limitations don't apply to him. The rest of us each have one life with 24 hours in a day. We more or less accept the yoke of time. In so doing we can find self-definition and, eventually, some sense of purpose. But in narcissism nothing can be excluded, hence, nothing can be truly chosen. Time is narcissism's greatest adversary because its limits cannot, ultimately, be avoided.

The context of the treatment of narcissistic issues is the patient's growing awareness of time. Time forces us to see that this life *does* count. Biological clocks keep ticking, whether or not we pay attention. Stalling eventuates in being closed out of some options.

This makes the treatment of narcissism especially fraught with conflicting injunctions for the clinician. On one hand, the demands of neutrality require that the analyst refrain from a cheerleader position, coaxing the patient into a life. On the other hand, a determination to stall life also stalls the treatment. The patient who won't recognize what she has and has not done with her life can't self-reflect much in treatment. This puts the analyst in the painful position of failing at his job. He often loses track of its purpose, feels ashamed that he is fraudulently posing as an analyst, but really accomplishing nothing. In short, this work brings out the clinician's potential for narcissistic difficulties.

Of course we, like everyone else, have individual reactions to the experience of failure. Some of us try to cover it up. In treatment this might result in analyst and patient engaging in years of "busywork" or becoming adept at distracting themselves, and each other, from the fact that the patient's life is going by. Some of us are angered by the feeling of failure and need to blame someone. Our literature provides us with convenient rationales for why it was all the patient's fault. We develop theories to explain why "borderline" and "narcissistic" patients are too difficult, not suitable candidates for the kind of treatment we provide (Epstein, 1979). This may help the clinician avoid a shameful sense of inadequacy, but if the treatment has circled for years without addressing the patient's unlived life, nothing can bring back his lost opportunities.

The treatment's location in the span of the analyst's life is also worth reflection. I know I am not the same, personally or professionally, as I was 20 years ago. Life, relationships, and time itself are different experiences for me, and I am sure that affects my work. What I notice, focus on, fail to hear, respond to, let pass in silence, express in the first person, tire of, am willing to break the frame for, meet with passion, and fight, speaks volumes about me. It reflects where I am in my own life, and "where I am" is, at least in part, about time.

Thus for both treatment participants, locating in time lends meaning to the moment and purpose to the hour.

Transcending Time

In an endlessly fascinating sense, treatment must be both time-bound and free of time's constraints. It both exists and does not exist in a particular time and space. It lives within time's constraints and also transcends them.

Transcending time is, I believe, one of the sources of joy for human beings. In a previous paper (Buechler, 2002a), I tried to describe the "transcendent joy" we all feel when we overcome a limitation. Watching a film, we root for heroes to leap over obstacles. We love the moment of "takeoff," the bursting through boundaries that signals freedom. I know of no more beautiful expression of this feeling than Wilbur's poem "The Writer," which tells the story of a father transfixed, listening intently outside the door while his daughter tries to write. He waits, hopeful that he will hear the clacking typewriter that would signal his daughter has found words. Listening at the door he recalls:

> I remember the dazed starling
> Which was trapped in that very room, two years ago;
> How we stole in, lifted a sash
>
> And retreated, not to affright it;
> And how for a helpless hour, through the crack of the
>   door,
> We watched the sleek, wild, dark
>
> And iridescent creature
> Batter against the brilliance, drop like a glove
> To the hard floor, or the desk-top,
> And wait then, humped and bloody,
>
> For the wits to try it again; and how our spirits
> Rose when, suddenly sure,
> It lifted off from the chair-back,

Beating a smooth course for the right window
And clearing the sill of the world.

It is always a matter, my darling,
Of life or death, as I had forgotten. I wish
What I wished you before, but harder [Wilbur, 1989, pp. 23–24].

Our hearts leap when we clear "the sill of the world." There is a thrill in transcending the obstacles that generally limit us. Time is a significant example of such an obstacle. That is why, I believe, we feel joy when we "lose ourselves" in an activity. It is the joy, in a Winnicottian (Winnicott, 1971) sense, of letting go of keeping track of time. We fly free of time, "clearing the sill of the world."

It is a grave problem, it seems to me, when a person can't transcend time. When unmoored joy is unavailable, for whatever reason, a significant source of joy is lost. In narcissism, for example, we can never lose ourselves. We are true cynics, seeing our own self-absorption everywhere we look. The only aims worth striving for are those that enhance us. This robs the self of the experience of transcendence. Even in our most creative or playful or generous acts, our self-concern ties us down. We are isolationists—only really caring about what lies within our own borders. Around us we see only other isolationists. In the world this creates, it is difficult to have any abiding purpose.

Once again, I see it as part of the analyst's task to differ meaningfully with this isolationism in our actions, not, necessarily, in words. We manifest the transcendence of time clinically in ways that allow us to convey a sense of purpose. *We lose ourselves in the work in front of the patient.* I tried to describe this process in a paper (2002a, p. 617) on joy:

> As an analyst, my office, the patient, and my own mind often exist in a kind of transitional space. Like the child's experience of the blanket, my experience is unbound by the usual limitations. I am any age, we are anywhere, it is any time.
>
> Of course, this is not the only truth. Just as the blanket has a size, in the treatment hour I still have an identity. But my awareness of it is intermittent. There are moments when I lose myself in the feel of the work. The patient and I are not bound by our histories and self-definitions. We are two instances of life.

When I can be an instance of life, free of the constraints of time, place, and identity, I can manifest how precious this freedom is. I can also convey the interpenetrating nature of human experience—that we are many, and one; here now, and everywhere we have ever been. I can express *in action* how we shape and become each other, the genuinely interpersonal nature of human existence.

Thus, I believe it is vital for us, as analysts, to locate in time *and* transcend it. In manifesting both of these aspects of being human, we find purpose.

Losing Meaning

The painter Wassily Kandinsky once said each brush stroke should come from "inner necessity." When we lose the pull of inner necessity entirely, life grows empty of purpose. As analysts, when our work loses a sense of purpose, we have capitulated to burnout.

Generally, as human beings, we gain some sense of purpose from our interpersonal connections. We want to provide well for our children, or have impact on our students, or earn to help our partners, or contribute to our community, political party, church, and so on. We make emotional investments of time, effort, care. They pay us back in that we gain convicted purpose, self-definition, inner momentum, and self-respect. When we lose interpersonal connections, we forfeit this source of a sense of purpose.

Specifically, as analysts, we risk burnout when we try too hard to engage every patient, regardless of the obstacles. Particularly young, relatively inexperienced analysts often put themselves out to try to please the patient, bending the frame, extending their availability, suppressing all interpretations that might narcissistically injure. The analyst may approach the session with great anxiety, so worried about saying the wrong thing that he can hardly speak, or promising to fulfill the patient's needs whether or not this is possible. Eventually the patient makes one too many demands for extra time or other special concessions. The clinician, fed up, may then become punitive or self-punitive, depending on his own character issues. He may find a way to dismiss the patient abruptly. As A. Cooper (1986) warned, these forays in therapeutic sainthood may lead us to burn out relatively early in our careers.

Burnout is a terrible loss. It is a loss of faith in the profession and in oneself. The burned-out analyst may feel she has to continue practicing for economic or other reasons, but it has become an empty exercise. Continuing to go through the motions can further demoralize us.

I tried to describe (2000, p. 87) one possible understanding of the use of burnout as a defense:

> In burnout, it is as though making the work not matter could offer solace, relief from repetitive experiences of stress, pain and loss. If what I'm doing has no meaning, then losing patients and the discouraging climate would not hurt so much. Unconsciously, cynicism offers an illusion of protection from pain. Better to deaden oneself than to be continually assaulted by loss. Of course, this is not a real solution, and the burnt-out analyst has suffered the greatest possible loss—the loss of faith in the worthwhileness of what he can accomplish.

Regardless of its causes, burnout cripples us in that we become unable to convey a sense of purpose because we no longer feel this conviction ourselves. To my mind burnout is the greatest professional loss we can suffer. The absence of purpose in burnout can serve as yet another indication of how vital the sense of purpose is, to the health of our work and to our own emotional well-being.

6   *Creating Emotional Balance*

She is the life of any party, bar, or family event. She wears tight, skimpy clothes; large, expensive jewelry; heavy makeup. Her lithe body conveys a surplus of nervous energy, a constant fidget. On her bad days she enters sessions warning me to watch out, and peppers the hour with barely veiled suicide threats. Her life story, as she tells it, is a series of calamities. Her family, friends, and many physicians often sound like caricatures, reminding me of Honoré Daumier's satiric sculptures of self-important officials. Some want nothing to do with her, others fall instantly in love, but she never fails to make an impression.

Beth personifies unstable, intense affect. When she is angry with me, rage permeates her body, the room, and my own consciousness. When she is amused, she is a bubbly champagne, infallibly intoxicating. Like an infant she is entirely in the grip of her emotions and conveys them in an intense, distilled form. It is like being with the most unsoothable baby, a concentrated ball of pure affect.

Although slender, Beth seems to spill all over. She is a frequent presence in the sessions of patients before and after her hour, an unwelcome intrusion to some, an amusing sideshow to others. To me, she can be funny, outrageous, sweet, exhausting, frustrating, enraging, frightening. Anything but boring.

I sometimes feel it would be easy to miss her ongoing suffering and get caught up in her vivid self-presentation. But I know Beth is genuinely unhappy much of the time.

Like Bollas's patient Jane (1987, pp. 191–192), discussed in chapter 3, Beth elicits a split between a part of me caught up in today's "event" and another part concerned about her in an ongoing sense. Her affective intensity and sudden shifts combine to make her presence disruptive. It is too easy to get swept into her whirlwind.

Sherby (1989) describes the positive aspect of this affective climate for the analyst:

> About six months ago a colleague asked why I was particularly interested in treating borderline patients. Without hesitation I replied, "The intensity!" Working with borderlines is never dull. From one hour to the next, indeed, sometimes from one minute to the next, the content, process and accompanying affect of therapy are constantly changing. It is what makes the borderline's world chaotic and tumultuous, but can make the therapist's experience rich and varied. The analyst is intensely involved in the therapeutic process. Whether raged against or clung to there is never any doubt that the analyst matters. There is never the feeling of insignificance, or even nonexistence which one may experience in treating schizoid or obsessive-compulsive patients [p. 574].

I believe part of the challenge of working with Beth is my resolving the internal splits she elicits in me well enough to serve as an adequate model. She often worries me, and I have to register alarm and, at the same time, trust her. I have to hold both of these responses openly enough to communicate vividly what jugglers humans are.

Harold Searles (1986) has given us a real taste of the impact of unintegrated affect:

> One woman patient said, "I can't tell you how much I love you or how much of a shit I think you are." In saying, "how much I love you," her affective tone was one of glowingly unambivalent love; but in saying only moments later, "how much of a shit I think you are," her affect was unambivalently one of hostile contempt [pp. 500–501].

Searles's intensely humane attitude is well conveyed in this passage:

My own clinical and supervisory experience strongly indicates to me that there are certain intense, and intensely difficult, feelings which the therapist can be expected to develop in response to the patient's development of the transference-borderline-psychosis. It may well be that, as the years go on, we shall become able to do psychoanalytic therapy with borderline and schizophrenic patients with increasing success in proportion to our ability to accept that, just as it is to be assumed an inherent part of the work that the *patient* will develop a transference-borderline-psychosis or transference-psychosis, it is also to be assumed no less integrally that the *therapist* will develop—hopefully, to a limited, self-analytically explorable degree, appreciably sharable with the patient—an area of countertransference-borderline-psychosis or even countertransference psychosis. It should be unnecessary to emphasize that going crazy, whole hog, along with the patient will do no good and great harm. But I believe that we psychoanalytic therapists collectively will become, through the years, less readily scared and better able to take up this work and pursue it as a job to be done relatively successfully, as we become proportionately able, forthrightly and unashamedly, to take the measure of feelings we can *expect* ourselves to come to experience, naturally, in the course of working with these patients [pp. 510–511].

Interestingly, Searles is emphasizing the *normalcy* of the analyst's intense, even psychotic experience with the "borderline" patient. He suggests that if we accept and expect this experience, we will be able to work better. But he is locating the source of change differently from where I would assign it. Searles believes if the patient is allowed his craziness, he will eventually overcome it. We help, in effect, by sharing and thereby detoxifying psychotic functioning. I would say we help more through how we relate to pulls toward splitting. I must register Beth's urgency *and* keep hold of a calming long-term perspective. I want the patient to become truly himself but also to emerge from a path toward psychosis.

Briefly, the concept of emotional balance has three major conceptual consequences for me:

1. It leads me to a particular understanding of empathy, as a compensatory process. This is close in spirit to Kohut's (1984) thinking. Empathy is not accurate registering and mirroring of emotions. It is an emotional balancing on the analyst's part with which the patient comes to identify. Thus, with a patient in a rage, for example, I begin to feel my version of his intense rage. In me this elicits anticipatory guilt, about the possibly hurtful impact of my rage. The patient comes to identify with my anticipatory guilt, which calms his rage. Thus, in the empathic process I feel my version of his rage, and he feels his version of my anticipatory guilt. I don't feel his rage and he doesn't feel my guilt. We each bring our own lifelong style of experiencing each of the basic human emotions to every new situation.

2. This leads to a conception of therapeutic action centered on modulating intense emotions with other intense emotions, not, generally, with verbal formulations. With Beth, for example, my calm is an "interpretation" of her urgency, without any words (necessarily) being spoken.

3. This reformulates some notions of defense. Defense can be seen as an attempt to deal with intense affect. It differs in form, depending on the person's character style *and* the principal emotion involved. For example, some people will mostly project their intense emotions. They may be especially likely to project feelings that would otherwise create shame and guilt in them. But they might be less likely to project their loneliness (a more fully elaborated discussion of defense is offered later in this chapter).

Thus, the concept of emotional balance leads to a particular view of empathy, therapeutic action, and defense. It also has implications for how we define emotional health and pathology.

What, exactly, needs to change in Beth? Is it the sheer intensity of affect, or the speed of affective shifts, or the particular combinations of affect, or the relationship between thought and affect, or something else? Variously described in the literature as hysterical (Chodoff, 1974; Lionells, 1986, 1995), borderline (Kernberg, 1975; Sherby, 1989), or narcissistic (Kohut, 1971; Fiscalini, 1995), these highly emotional patients capture our attention, evoke our concern, and provoke our impatience, while also often touching our hearts.

To understand Beth's unsettling impact on me and to formulate what would help her, I have to have a conception of healthy emotional functioning. I need a model of ideal emotionality to envision Beth's "progress." Would a healthier Beth feel emotions less intensely? Would she express them in a more modulated fashion? In short, how would she experience and express affect differently?

Among the many possible topics we could derive from this case description, I briefly address only six:

1. The slippery concept of emotional normalcy.
2. The frequent failure to identify specific emotions when analysts, clinical theoreticians, and even researchers study emotional responsiveness.
3. The concept that emotions are often more powerful in modulating other emotions than any cognition, by itself, would be.
4. The changes this emotion-driven perspective suggests in our traditional analytic conceptions of neutrality, abstinence, therapeutic action, resistance, and so on.
5. The changes this would suggest in how we understand case material.
6. How this conception of healthy emotionality affects the clinician's use of clinical theory (dealt with more fully in chapter 9).

Defining Normal Emotionality

A man faces extreme danger without any observable fear. A woman becomes hysterical because her haircut looks "wrong." A man becomes violently angry at his wife because she interrupts him. A child feels too much self-conscious shame to join his classmates on stage at graduation. A man feels no interest or excitement toward his wife. Which reactions are pathological and worthy of psychological treatment?

A frequent topic for me is the issue of the clinician's (often unarticulated) theory of healthy and abnormal emotionality. How depressed can we be and still be considered normal? How much speedy excitement qualifies as manic? What kind of anxiety gets diagnosed? Which emotional patterns create an impression of hysteria? When is the absence of an emotion pathological? How much rage can a parent show a child and still be within normal limits?

Each clinician brings an often unexamined "theory" of healthy and pathological emotionality to her work with patients. Some see intensity as key to differentiating normal from abnormal feelings. Others rely on a sense of the "appropriateness" of emotional behavior. For some the health of a person's emotional system depends mainly on how their affects and cognitions interact (Barnett, 1980). Does thought shape the expression of the individual's emotions? Or do affects tumble out, unmodulated by cognition? Some are swayed more by the effect of the subject's emotions on others. For example, some clinicians diagnose "borderline" rage mainly on the basis of their countertransferential experience (Epstein, 1979).

The "theory" of healthy emotionality that we bring to our work deeply affects our focus in the session, our notion of treatment goals, and our countertransference reactions to the patient. Of myriad possibilities, we pick up on what stands out *to us.* I think my own view of healthy emotionality shapes what, in a session, I don't even notice, because I take it as commonplace. This has a tremendous impact on the course of the work.

I am generally not content with considering "cure" as meaning muting the intensity of affect. This treats emotion as a "problem" rather than as a resource. Furthermore, it does not adequately differentiate the emotions, some of which may themselves be playing a vital role modulating other affects. It is important, to me, not to "homogenize" or pathologize emotion (Spiegel, 1980; Buechler, 1997, 2000). Sadness, for example, is a normal human response to loss and should not be equated with depression.

We each bring our life experience, our insight derived from training, reading, and our own treatment, to these questions. We have a personal "take" on normal emotionality in everyday life and on normal emotional reactions to traumatic events. Furthermore, we have often unarticulated beliefs about how children should be taught to deal with their feelings and how feelings change in treatment and in the rest of life. Perhaps most significantly, we have a set of beliefs about normal emotionality in clinicians during sessions. There are emotional responses we would probably all consider outside that range, such as becoming uncontrollably, violently angry. But less extreme reactions may be less clear. For instance some of us are more comfortable crying with patients than others.

The concept of emotional normalcy is elusive. I think this is so partly because we each began to formulate our own personal version prespeech. We each have a sense of what we mean by an acceptable emotional response, but we often find this hard to communicate or to formulate.

Beth's vivacity can be seen as charming, or annoying (but within normal limits), or symptomatic. Has fortune smiled on Beth if she has found an analyst whose everyday emotional patterns closely match her own? More generally, is Beth better off if her analyst is of her gender, and from a culture similar to hers in its assumptions about healthy affect? Are there identifiable "truths" about normal human emotional behavior, or is everything in the eye (and personal predilections) of the beholder?

Child-rearing practices can be used as a barometer of the ideal of emotionality prevalent in a culture and era. Parents told to let their infants cry themselves to sleep, those told sparing the rod could spoil the child, and those advised to feed on demand are being encouraged to adopt very different stances toward their child's emotionality. Dickens's comic masterpiece *Hard Times* (1954) comments on the sad results of negative attitudes toward childrens' feelings. Imaginative curiosity is to be rooted out, hunted down, and punished with shame in the world Dickens portrayed. Perhaps no society has been as vicious as Dickens imagined, but some social groups can greatly discourage emotional display, as Tomkins (1962, 1963) describes with his conception of the "socialization" of the emotions.

Emotional Specificity

To be useful, any clinical or theoretical discussion has to specify the particular emotion being considered. There was a time when a patient's "emotionality" was treated as one-dimensional, as though anger, fear, joy, and so on were interchangeable. Patients were categorized as highly emotional or unemotional, and it was assumed that an individual who experienced and expressed a high intensity of one emotion would feel and express the other affects intensely, too. Although this may often be the case, it fails to attend to nuances of difference in an individual's emotional experience.

By asking exactly what a patient felt and pursuing whether, for example, it was shame or guilt, fear or anxiety, anger or hate, we make the statement that it matters to be specific about the emotion. Thus we can encourage the patient's development of a more subtle language for discriminating among the affects (Spiegel, 1980; Buechler, 1993, 1997).

Emotions Modulating Other Emotions

We distract infants from pain, counting on interest and curiosity to overpower distress. Anger overcomes shame and shyness, as we publicly denounce a political outrage. We resist a temptation to avoid guilt. We mobilize to protect those we love, surmounting our fears. In countless ways we rely on emotions to modulate other emotions. Although cognition (insight) may play an important role, emotions are often powerful in altering other affects. In my experience, this usually occurs outside awareness. We don't usually formulate strategies for dealing with our feelings, but we instinctively gravitate toward affect to handle other affects.

A patient confronts her own absorption in past injustices. She realizes how much time and energy she has spent denouncing the offenders. One day she angrily announces that she isn't going to give "them" even one more day of her life! Her anger at the waste of her time is fueling her determination to make better use of the present and future.

Examples abound of emotions modulating other affects. This is happening in both treatment participants. Sometimes the clinician can use her awareness of how she is maintaining some emotional balance in her effort to help the patient find an equilibrium (see the earlier discussion of empathy).

Passionate Analytic Terminology

Terms such as *neutrality, abstinence, transference, countertransference, the analytic attitude, defense,* and *the goals of psychoanalysis* can be understood differently with concepts from emotion theory in mind. Looking at fundamental analytic issues this way can allow us to drop much of our jargon and use experience-near language. We can talk about shame, rage, sadness, and other experiences we have all had. We can understand empathy, therapeutic action, and defense in evocative emotional terms. As I have suggested, this can promote greater dialogue with other disciplines and encourage analysts and analytic candidates to use a broader range of life experience in their work.

Neutrality and Abstinence

Often confused, these two concepts are key components of analytic technique. Analytic neutrality has been described as an inner state in the analyst (Jacobs, 1986):

The analytic idea of neutrality is a highly complex one. It involves not only a way of listening that receives with impartiality material deriving from each of the psychic agencies and a technical approach that eschews the resolution of conflict through influence in favor of interpretations, but it implies in the analyst a state of receptivity that can accomplish these goals. The proper use of neutrality as a technical measure requires a considerable degree of inner "neutrality," that is, a state of mind in which ego functions necessary for analytic work are not impaired by conflict [p. 297].

Elsewhere (Buechler, 1999), I have suggested some difficulties inherent in the clinical use of this concept. Briefly, they include the following:

1. Neutrality implies that the analyst can maintain an even focus on material coming from the patient's id, ego, and superego (A. Freud, 1936; Jacobs, 1986). This does not seem possible, given the analyst's inevitable investment in health. Struggling with this issue, Poland (1984) wondered, "Can an analyst truly interpret without trivializing unless he selects some issues as more related to anxiety, to defense, to inhibitions, than others? Can an analyst in practice truly deal with a perversion as if it were not a constricted and symptomatic compromise formation?" (p. 297).

2. If neutrality is taken to mean holding countertransference feelings in check, this would deny the analyst the expression of passions crucial to the work. The analyst's emotional openness can play a vital role in helping the patient fight depression and distinguish his interpersonal intentions from his actual impact. The analyst will not be able to provide a "relational challenge" (Buechler, 1999) without expressing feelings. That is, to contrast sufficiently with the patient's transferential expectations, the analyst will have to respond affectively. This contrast is essential to clarifying what the patient generally expects. Greenberg (1991) has explored the issue of how much the analyst should be an old versus a new object, arguing for a tension between the two. While the words used in the analyst's interpretations should neutrally invite the patient's full self-expression, the analyst's passionate manner is crucial to inspiring hope, communicating urgency about time and the preciousness of life, and promoting affective modulation. Without affective expression we could not, for example, be effective in

communicating on many levels at once how loss can be borne (see chapter 7).

3. The analyst's values inevitably affect what she hears, doesn't hear, responds to, is willing to confront, and so on. Perception and focus can't be neutral. Consequently, the analyst can't merely follow the unfolding material because her own focusing inevitably directs it.

In 1915, Freud declared that the "treatment must be carried out in abstinence." Mitchell (1993) takes a clear position on the problems with this dictum:

> Similarly, the principle of "abstinence" enshrined in classical theory of technique is probably one of the most effective ways to ensure that some patients never work through childhood longings. The longing is ostensibly given up through a process of rational conversion (subjecting the unconscious wish to "secondary process"), but there is a sad, wistful quality to this disciplined "maturity" and abstinence. The analyst's willingness to try out the patient's solution, when possible, can open up another very different experience [pp. 185–186].

If our aim is to clarify the longing, which is more effective: deprivation or satisfaction? One fundamental problem with learning from deprivation is that what is learned often differs from what was intended. The patient from whom we withhold approval may "learn" less about his longing than about his analyst's method, character, or both. Abstinence is a kind of Rorschach test, inviting projection. The deprived child may "learn" that his wishes were bad, that he is bad or unloved, that he has parents incapable of love, and so on. Similarly, the patient may take unintended meanings from the experience of analytic abstinence.

Abstinence, in other words, is limited in what it can communicate emotionally. It is a one-dimensional, flat, predetermined response. It is too unvarying and too proscribed to communicate the analyst's process about *this* patient's specific wishes today. The patient denied approval based on the principle of abstinence doesn't learn, for example, that he might get a better response if he didn't demand so clamorously.

This is not an argument for gratification of patients' wishes but rather one against reflexive abstinence because of the potentially informative emotional interchange it precludes. The patient who seeks guidance on Monday and Thursday and gets more on Thursday has an interpersonal opportunity. He can work with his analyst on why that happened. What was different? Can the analyst introspectively find what made the request feel different to her? Did she, for example, feel on Thursday that the patient was overcoming a longstanding fear of dependency by asking for help? Did that influence her toward gratification? What can both participants learn from this?

The patient whose longing for approval is denied on the basis of abstinence won't learn much about interpersonal negotiations. He won't learn that how he expresses need matters. He won't learn the disappointment we can feel after getting what we wished for. Shame and guilt about the need, or envy of the analyst for being able to gratify, won't occur. Neither will joy, curiosity about the analyst's process, fear of losing the approval, hope for more in the future, and so on.

Both neutrality and abstinence can rob treatment of the power of the emotional interchange. As absolute rules, both are too limiting and rigid. The passionate neutrality I believe in maintains a tension between the wording of interpretations, which neutrally invites the patient's free self-expression, and a passionate manner that instigates sufficient urgency and hope.

Although I don't believe abstinence as a reflexive stance is clinically viable, I do think a related concept can be useful. Freud (1926) believed in maintaining an "optimal" level of anxiety in the patient. Sullivan (1953, 1954), I think, had a similar notion. I would say moderate intensities of all the emotions allow the work of the treatment to proceed. This includes moderate levels, in the analyst and in the patient, of curiosity, loneliness, sadness, and many other affects. Thus I would argue for a stance that constantly monitors these levels. Too much gratification would skew this balance just as easily as too little. The patient whose curiosity is gratified with enticing personal information about the analyst may become gluttonous. She may feel as overstimulated as a child exposed to explicit sexual behavior. A balance is upset. The motivating power of a degree of unfulfilled hunger is lost.

The patient denied all gratification, on the basis of abstinence, may become too lonely to continue the work. Paradoxically, a measure meant to maintain the analytic frame destroys it. This may be one way to understand what happened to Freud's patient Dora. Perhaps she was given so little support for her point of view (about her family, etc.) that she was too lonely with Freud to continue their work.

Our aim has to be enough curiosity, hope, and good will to maintain ongoing work. Adequate levels of anger (at the waste of life), fear (of future regrets), and other emotions often play important roles. Perhaps some loneliness is necessary and inevitable, but it can't be so intense that it is disruptive. The same may be said of anxiety, sadness, and shame.

In short, although I believe there is a place for a modified version of neutrality, I feel abstinence is too restrictive. I also believe that both treatment participants need the motivating power that moderate levels of many emotions provide. For treatment to thrive, neither participant can be so frustrated that their curiosity is shut down. It is part of our analytic task to struggle with, and titrate, our own emotional balance as we also learn about and help to modulate the patient's. In each treatment we have to continually redefine what constitutes a moderate level of each emotion. Within the context of *this* patient at *this* moment of our work, what would moderate shame be, for me? How can I regain it?

Transference–Countertransference as Endless Mourning

The patient and I have come to expect the usual story to repeat. She embarks on a new friendship with another woman. At first it seems to promise much-needed companionship, but it is not long before good will frays in familiar ways. An ungenerous act, a falling out, weeks of estrangement, prideful reluctance to share in the apologies, then the petering out, until they settle into permanent absence in each other's lives.

It still hurts, even though each instance slides quickly into its category now. We recognize the "mother thing" as it is happening, rather than afterward. The pain of it is muted compared with earlier episodes. The theme is played out in miniature between us, as disappointments.

The most interesting part is that these episodes began long before her mother died. This tremendous loss seemed to have no impact on the pattern. Various names would fit this repetition. I could call it transference in the sense Greenberg (1991) has suggested:

> Transference can be optimally creative only when the patient
> can be playful with it—only, that is, when he can experience any

particular reaction as reflecting but one part of a vast range of possibilities. This depends on the freedom to be aware of as many transference paradigms as possible. The process is similar to what I have discussed as the capacity to experience previously repressed re-representations; the description points the way to what I think of as the genuinely therapeutic analysis of transference [p. 239].

I think it is more clinically useful to see this as a kind of rite. The ungenerous mother, only an aspect of this patient's maternal experience, is repeatedly revisited because she could never be accepted and commemorated. She caused too much grief and confusion; she contradicted too many better moments.

These are the figures who never settle into their graves but endlessly inhabit our daily lives (Loewald, 1960). Rest is denied them. They cannot be definitively mourned because our anger interferes with the necessary inner object tie. Mourning is only partially a letting go. It is equally a continuance of an inner object relationship (Gaines, 1997; Buechler, 2000). When the actual interchange was too ambivalent, contradictory, or confusing, however, the process gets stuck and, like a scratched record, keeps repeating at the marred spot. Repeating the undigestible element is the only way to remember. Restless ghosts are always awaiting their next chance at life. Thus transference is how we mark the unmournable aspects of those we have known. In this sense, countertransference does not differ from transference. The analyst's ghosts, stirred by the patient's material, simply find a new embodiment.

It has always seemed unrealistic to me to say that a transference is "fully resolved." The emotions may become much less violent. The pattern may be much more reluctant to assert itself. The issues are less salient. But I don't believe its potential for repetition ever ends. I hope ungiving mothers take up less of my patient's life in the future. But for her some anger and sorrow and some puzzled tears are part of life.

The Analytic Attitude as New Experience

A desirable degree of subordination of personality will be evident in the analyst's remaining curious, eager to find out, and open to surprise. It will be evident also in the analyst's taking

nothing for granted (without being cynical about it), and remaining ready to revise conjectures or conclusions already
arrived at, tolerate ambiguity or incomplete closure over extended periods of time, accept alternative points of view of the
world, and bear and contain the experiences of helplessness,
confusion, and aloneness that not infrequently mark periods
of analytic work with each analysand [Schafer, 1983, p. 7].

When have most of us known someone like that in our personal
lives? How often do we encounter someone brave enough to bear uncertainty and selfless enough to try to see us without personally preferred preconceptions? How many people will tolerate being lost to
help us feel found?

The "analytic attitude," Schafer's ideal (1983) of therapeutic participation, is a new experience for most people. In that sense it may,
paradoxically, differ from what Greenberg (1991, p. 217) recommended—that the analyst should be, in equal measure, the old transference object and a new interpersonal experience.

If we achieve an analytic attitude, we are presenting a fundamentally novel interpersonal opportunity. We are curious, willing to be surprised, and unhampered by narcissistic needs of our own. Most
significantly the paranoid element that often plays some role in human
theory building (see chapter 1) does not limit us—there is nothing we
need to see in a particular way. We are free of "memory and desire."
We have no point to prove.

Although this has obvious advantages, it seems to me that its main
impact would be as a model of a novel way of being in the world. It
shows the patient the value of openness to new experience, which is the
essence of mental health that Sullivan proposed (1953, 1954, 1956). An
analytic attitude manifests a curious, exploratory way to be human. It
comments on the patient's predicament in a unique way. Unlike the attitude of anyone else the patient is likely to have known, it says everything about the patient is more interesting than infuriating, more
surprising than shocking. It selflessly examines and compares without
intense envy getting in the way. It contains contagious anxiety rather
than being contaminated by it.

Perhaps children need an early period of protection from painful
realities. Maybe we all need to start in a fairy-tale land so that we can
become strong enough to bear life. In this sense, the open analyst, like a

sweet fairy godmother or a mythically heroic father, prepares us for the real world.

The Joy of Splitting

Not infrequently, in my experience, patients come into treatment fearing that they will be told how to "master" their emotions but will still really feel the same. This fear is justified. Much of our literature treats affect as a "beast" to be tamed by cognitive means. This fails to credit emotion with the power to modulate other emotions.

If we think of emotions as our most powerful tools for delimiting affective intensities, we emerge with a revised understanding of the defenses. It does not make sense to focus mainly on cognitive efforts to "master" instinctual and affective pulls, as has been traditionally held. Defenses have been seen as mainly cognitive techniques that the ego makes use of in conflicts that can lead to neurosis (Freud, 1926; A. Freud, 1966). Anna Freud (1966, p. 44) named 10 defenses (regression, repression, reaction formation, isolation, undoing, projection, introjection, turning against the self, reversal, and sublimation). Most of these are explained as though it is cognition that generally alters affect (with some exceptions).

But if we assume emotions have tremendous power to alter other emotions, we would have to think of defenses as primarily affective efforts to maintain an emotional balance (perhaps not unlike Kohut's, 1977, "compensatory structures"). Defenses then become attempts to use mainly emotional means to delimit the eruption of profound shame, anxiety, guilt, fear, depression, anger, distress, or sadness. In their effort to maintain balance, defenses would also respond to threats to positive affects, such as joy and curiosity.

We all develop a personal history of experience of each of the basic human emotions (Izard, 1977; Buechler, 1993) and a personal affective style. For example, I may be particularly shame-prone, react to shame with heightened anxiety, and often defensively modulate it with heightened curiosity. I cannot help bringing this emotional "signature" to my work as an analyst, as I bring it to all other aspects of my life. My goal is to use my style's potential resources in *this* moment with *this* patient. In the best-case scenario, my analytic training has acquainted me well with the pitfalls and strengths of my particular emotional makeup. It has facilitated my ability to distinguish affective nuances (Spiegel, 1980; Buechler, 1997). But no training, no preparation guarantees that I will be able to cope with my next patient. I have to count on my own spontaneous, unpredictable emotional responses. This aspect of the work is not a consciously chosen "technique," although it has been exposed to many years of analytic and self-analytic effort. Nevertheless, my emotional responses in a session spring from real reactions and will generally conform to my emotional style.

This way of thinking about the curative potential of the emotional interplay in treatment seems to me similar in spirit to Daniel Stern's (1998) concept of treatment's effect on interpersonal procedural memory. It differs from Fonagy's views (2001) in that it relies less on (cognitive) reflection.

We can also think of emotional balancing in treatment as a way to address trauma therapeutically. If we have a broad perspective on the nature of trauma, it is a frequent experience in life. As Freud suggested (1926), anything that threatens to emotionally overwhelm us can be considered traumatic. Trauma is distressing because of its impact, regardless of its source. In Freud's words, "the essence of a traumatic situation is the experience of helplessness on the part of the ego in the face of accumulation of excitation, whether of external or internal origin" (p. 81). This means to me that any feeling so intense that it threatens balance is traumatic, at least to some degree.

I believe that treatment includes countless episodes of regaining emotional balance, for both participants. Balance may be (temporarily) lost to intense anger, fear, shame, curiosity, anxiety, and so on. If the analyst adequately manifests the process of using emotions to regain balance, some parts of this experience can be useful to the patient, who may integrate them into his emotional style. I emphasize that it is not always an "imitation" of the analyst's way of emotionally coping that helps the patient; it is often the experience of being with the analyst, as the analyst openly struggles for balance, that can be useful if the patient reformulates it to fit his own emotional style. Another way to say this is that intense emotionality is detoxified or detraumatized by the *experience* of being with the overtly and actively emotionally balancing analyst. Sometimes the patient mainly learns a way of balancing his own emotions, but at other times the experience of being near the analyst mainly allows the patient to feel what it is like interpersonally to be with someone who actively strives for emotional balance.

This differs from the usual conception of the work with defenses in the following ways:

1. Emotion is credited with the power to modulate other emotions.

2. Because the emotions form a system and the level of each emotion affects all the others, any heightened or lowered feeling will impinge on the whole system. Thus the individual may defend against diminished joy just as much as against shame or anxiety.

3. This way of thinking does not privilege anxiety over other painful emotions, as those of Freud (1926), Sullivan (1953), and others do. We defensively avoid other kinds of pain as much as we attempt to delimit anxiety.

4. Clinically we can address, for example, the patient who is defensively trying to avoid guilt by focusing on any affect, present or (seemingly) absent, sensing our own affective state, and struggling toward emotional balance. This means we do not have to get bogged down when the patient comes into treatment obsessively focused on his anger, his depression, or any other single emotion.

According to this perspective, a defense such as splitting is an attempt to keep emotions separated that are difficult for human beings to experience simultaneously. This difficulty is illustrated by a definition of joy. Joy may be seen (Izard, 1977) as a sense of serenity, with everything in place. No intensely clashing thoughts or feelings disturb us in this state.

To preserve our joy, we sometimes sacrifice complexity and nuance, narrowing our vision down to a one-dimensional perspective. In a sense, all defenses move toward decreased emotional complexity. Projecting, for example, may allow us to avoid some of the contradictory aspects of our own natures.

This positive view, that when one adaptation fails it is inherent in us to search for another, was beautifully captured by Kohut (1984): "Just as a tree will, within certain limits, be able to grow around an obstacle so that it can ultimately expose its leaves to the life-sustaining rays of the sun, so will the self in its developmental search abandon the effort to continue in one particular direction and try to move forward in another" (p. 205).

Certain defenses may be better suited for particular affective tasks. If we look at defenses that greatly rely on cognition, we see that affective intensity can be modulated by defenses that rely on altering focus, or defenses that primarily rely on altering the attribution of meaning. Repression, for example, may be an especially smooth way to avoid jolts of surprise. Projection may neatly rid us of potential guilt and shame, as well as other feelings. Defenses that control focus, such as dissociation, may be especially effective with anxiety, whereas defenses that rely on magic (e.g., undoing) may help us most with anger. Put another way, anger leads to cohesion, so that what we often need to defend against is not the cognitive effect of the anger but the *meaning* of feeling the emotion (via undoing, compartmentalization, intellectualization, etc.). Anxiety, however, as Sullivan suggested (1953), operates like a blow on the head. Adequate defense against anxiety requires more than magical transformation of meanings. It takes actual change in what is figure versus what is (at most) ground.

Yet emotion is not just acted on; it is also a powerful modulator. In a fury we "forget" other feelings. Whistling in the dark, joy may outbalance fear. Sullivan (1956) stuck a friend with a pin while the friend was deeply concentrating on something else; the friend didn't feel pain and anger at being stuck until after his deep curiosity had been satisfied. When we love someone (or something) we can often conquer fear. In each of these examples, and countless more, we don't just master an emotion. We feel it differently. It is this changed balance of emotional experience that is at the heart of the treatment process.

Analytic Goals

Freud's oft-quoted goal, of turning neurotic suffering into common human misery has always sounded gloomy to me. I think it stops short of appreciating the full magnitude of treatment's potential.

It is true that treatment cannot eliminate the felt impact of the inherently sad aspects of life. In that sense, some misery is inevitable. Treatment cannot, for example, obliterate the pain of profound loss.

But under fortunate circumstances treatment gives the patient greater access to the power of his own emotionality. I believe treatment should aim to do several things:

1. *Treatment should aim to nurture the patient's relationship to her own curiosity, joy, and capacity for surprise.* This can help the patient bear painful losses (see chapter 7) and other hurtful aspects of life. It can also help balance resistances.

2. *Treatment should aim to enhance the patient's ability to use potentially painful emotional experience as motivation and information.* In treatment part of what we do is help the patient derive motivating power from modulated anger, shame, and guilt (for example). Valuable information can be learned from fear, anxiety, sadness, and envy. Sadness can help us understand what is important. Feiner (1986) once defined envy as giving "shape to desire": the feeling of envy can be used to clarify what we want out of life.

3. *Through repeated experiences, treatment should aim to help the patient access curiosity* (chapter 1), *hope* (chapter 2), *kindness* (chapter 3), *courage* (chapter 4), *a sense of purpose* (chapter 5), *emotional balance* (this chapter), *the ability to bear loss* (chapter 7), *and integrity* (chapter 8). These moments cannot be planned in advance, but the analyst can have it in mind, for example, that he is with a fundamentally schizoid patient, so he should look for opportunities to work on his own, along with the patient's, despair. Or, with the narcissistic patient, the analyst might need to be on the lookout for the chance to live out something potentially useful about the sense of purpose. In the case of a primarily paranoid patient, the analyst might think about what he is doing to try to maintain an open, curious mind.

4. *Treatment should aim to clarify what is happening interpersonally.* None of these ideas precludes the necessity of verbal interpretation, but if our focus changes, we are likely to interpret differently. For example, if we see defense as an effort to maintain emotional balance, we look for and respond to aspects of a session that allow us to address that balance.

5. *Treatment should aim to help develop the patient's analytic attitude–a kind of curious stance in life that is useful during and after the treatment.*

To illustrate what it is like to apply this way of thinking, I will take clinical material familiar to us, Freud's case of Dora, and suggest how we could understand the case, emphasizing the emotions as fundamental to all human experience.

Emotional Balance in Freud's Treatment of Dora

How can we understand what happened between Freud and Dora if we think of emotions as the chief modulators of other emotions?

I have always thought of Dora's termination with Freud as analogous to Nora's exit from her "doll's house." In both, a woman refuses to accept being defined by someone's ultimately stifling theory of her. Freud's handling (some would say manhandling) of Dora has received endless attention (e.g., McCaffrey, 1984). What can we say about Freud and Dora from a point of view that emphasizes emotions modulating other affects?

Showalter (1993) says Freud felt that "in order for the therapy to work, the hysteric had to accept and believe the narrative of the analyst" (p. 318). Instead, Dora "flatly denied Freud's narrative embellishments of her story, would not accept his version of her activities and feelings, and either contradicted him or fell into stubborn silence. Finally she walked out on Freud by refusing to continue with therapy at all" (p. 319).   .

I think of Dora, both in her family and with Freud, as probably feeling anger, loneliness, and perhaps shame. I am sure we could make a case for other emotional possibilities, but these three seem to be especially likely. Freud envisioned the treatment as a kind of combat. I don't see how his formulation could fail to elicit anger and loneliness. Probably, when she entered treatment, Dora had some hope that Freud would understand her striving for further education, her wish to avoid a stifling conventional role, and her anger at the secrecy and covert bartering in her family. But when Freud insisted Dora see herself his way, I imagine she felt lonelier than ever and lost any hope she had for help from treatment. Shame would be a likely component of Dora's feelings because Freud saw exposing her sexual secrets as important to her "cure."

Consider the likelihood that a similar set of negative affects were stimulated within Dora's family and in her treatment with Freud. Perhaps had Freud been able to evoke more positive emotions, such as curiosity, to balance the negative, the outcome would have been different. But Freud's closed oedipal theory didn't elicit Dora's passionate curiosity enough to sustain the work.

From a point of view emphasizing affective balance, I would say that

1. Freud created a treatment that evoked the same negative emotions Dora felt in her family.

2. Freud failed to evoke powerful curiosity because his own thinking was too rigidly confined to his favored interpretive framework.

3. Freud failed to love Dora enough and elicit her love. This may sound paradoxical in that in his later formulation of the concept of transference, Freud (1916) saw part of the problem as the patient's love

for the analyst. It is a matter of what we each mean by "love." Whereas Freud often used "love" as synonymous with sexual attraction, I am suggesting that if Freud and Dora had been able to love each other better, they might have resolved this standoff. By love I mean "the active concern for the life and growth of that which we love" (Fromm, 1956, p. 24).

4. Joy was also missing in the treatment. Izard (1977) says receptive joy is "a state that is extremely difficult to describe, (is) a feeling of trust and acceptance of the surrounding world" (p. 86).

The story of Dora and Freud thus becomes a sad commentary on missing positive emotions, such as hope, curiosity, love, and joy that, when sufficiently present, can balance the negative affects the work recruits. When the conduct of the treatment reproduces the patient's essential life situation and therefore evokes the same fundamental negative emotions, a great deal of positive affect is necessary to create sufficient balance.

Could Freud have evoked enough love, joy, curiosity, and hope for the case to have ended differently? Although we can never know, one way to understand why this wasn't possible would be to see Dora and Freud as too much alike to create an emotional balance. Each focused on a "truth" that had to be seen, and each had a mind too closed to scamper with the other. Stubbornly unyielding, each put making a particular point ahead of working out a relationship. Perhaps too similarly to Dora's family experience, her treatment failed because the participants were too certain to be curious enough. As in Dora's family, so in the treatment, each participant had too instrumental a use for each other to be able to love freely.

For Freud, Dora was too much a means toward a theoretical end rather than an end in herself. Freud could not evoke enough hope or joy in Dora, and he could not truly inspire her trust. Without sufficient curiosity, love, joy, and hope, Dora's anger, shame, and loneliness propelled her to end a process of self-discovery that had only begun. What should we learn from Dora and Freud? That transference cannot be usefully interpreted when the treatment actually reproduces the patient's family situation? That the analyst must not be closed-minded if he wants the patient to open her mind to his ideas? That he has to manifest curiosity to sufficiently elicit it? That if the patient is terribly lonely in the treatment she will not be motivated to continue with it? That trying to force someone to accept an interpretation creates an unproductive affective climate that negates any potential benefit from the insight?

Freud wanted to believe that Dora, in leaving him, was really taking revenge on Herr K. The failure of the treatment was due to this being acted out rather than verbally expressed. Freud himself said that Dora acted an essential part of her recollections and fantasies instead of reproducing them in the treatment. I suggest that the treatment failed because Freud's need for Dora to prove his theory was too similar to her family's uses of her, leaving her too ashamed, angry, and lonely and not enough heartened by hope, joy, curiosity, and love.

Maintaining Emotional Balance

To summarize, clinical use of emotion theory often involves capturing what we may instinctively already grasp from our own life experience. Many people may not know that differential emotion theory labels curiosity a fundamental emotion and may not think of the emotions as forming a system, with alterations in any one emotion affecting the levels of all the others. But most of us will try to interest a crying baby in a colorful toy. We "know" intensified curiosity can delimit distress.

Similarly clinicians may instinctively postpone confrontation with a patient, sidestepping narcissistic injury until the relationship has had time to build. We "know" hope, curiosity, and love can outweigh anger and hurt, if given a chance.

Patients often come to treatment hoping to change how they feel. They want more joy, hope, love, and interest and less anger, fear, anxiety, shame, guilt, and distress. But emotions cannot be "adjusted" up or down like a thermostat. We may not be able to alter directly the emotion we would like to change. We can't will ourselves to feel less anger. Clinicians often get lost, along with their patients, obsessively involved in trying to "fix" the patient's anger or anxiety or depression or sorrow. But we often can help people live in a way that maximizes their curiosity, for example, and this will affect their anger, sadness, fear, and so on.

The concept of emotional balance means the following to me:

1. Clinically I can try to have an impact on *any* emotion the patient feels in order to affect the whole system. When a patient comes to treatment despairing, I don't have to get lost with the patient, trying

to decrease the despair. I can focus on another emotion that may be less difficult to change at that time.

2. How someone lives has to change before she can cognitively understand why she lived as she did previously. Behavioral change often precedes insight in the sense that it creates a different emotional balance, and this contrast with the old balance opens the way to insight. For example, a patient who was very socially inhibited dares to risk more interpersonally. Experiences she then has may teach her why she was so inhibited in the first place. The initial "experiment" may have been an act of courage and hope. A bit of experience may lead to decreased fear of shame. In this less fearful state, even more can be risked. Taking interpersonal chances, the patient better understands her previous fears. The emotional balance has shifted, and new experiences are more likely.

3. Emotions modulate other emotions more powerfully, on the whole, than do cognitive insights. For example, genuinely curious about ourselves, we are less likely to get fixated on how everything wrong with a situation is someone else's "fault."

The clinician is just as vulnerable to emotional shifts as the patient. In chapter 9, I address how clinicians use theory to try to maintain their own emotional balance. For now I emphasize that we often have our greatest clinical impact through what we do to maintain ourselves emotionally. Patients watch us lose our patience and regain it. They hear our frustration and feel our sorrow. They see us momentarily lose and then regain our clinical spirit of inquiry. We take up our task, again, in September, or after vacations or other breaks. The pleasures and challenges, the hope to have an impact, the belief in the human spirit and in ourselves all reassert themselves. We don't get rid of anxiety, frustration, sorrow. Like any other human being, all the emotions affect us. We use all our curiosity, all our love for life, all our potential for joy in balancing whatever must be borne. It is inevitable that how we personally recover from moments of shame will be manifested at some point in the work. Patients see us lost and sense how we bear it. Intuitively they can feel what brings us joy and how that joy sustains us. They understand when they are loved, and when love is the only force strong enough to keep us fighting for more life.

7   *Bearing Loss*

In what I think of as one of the most moving passages in literature (*King Lear,* act V, scene 3, lines 305–307), Lear asks

> Why should a dog, a horse, a rat have life,
> And thou no breath at all?
> Thou'll come no more,
> Never, never, never, never, never!

Along with Lear we feel death's injustice, and we try to take in the un-
thinkable reality of "never." His beloved Cordelia, the daughter he
banished and so recently refound, is dead. The breath of life is forever
denied her, although it is bestowed on so many lesser creatures. How
do human beings take in such unfathomable enormities? That Cordelia, who had become so essential to Lear, is lost forever, that for her
there will be "no breath at all" is unbearable. Indeed, after trying to
deny her death Lear himself dies, seemingly unable to bear his pain.

How do we help people develop the strength to bear life's most
painful losses? I think of this capacity as a vital part of our emotional
equipment, along with curiosity, hope, kindness, courage, purpose,
emotional balance, and integrity. Each can be nurtured in psychoanalytic treatment.

I approach bearing loss with the premise that, most often, its sadness could be borne if it were not accompanied by other painful emotions. A vast literature addresses some of these combinations, while others have been relatively neglected, but may be equally significant in clinical practice. I am particularly interested in how loneliness, regret, shame, and despair complicate loss. But other modulating emotions make loss *more* bearable. How the treatment's life is lived, and especially how termination is lived, can make a difference.

Of course the voluminous literature on treating depression is relevant but will not be summarized here (for a review, from an interpersonal point of view, see Bose, 1995, and also Spiegel, 1960, 1965, 1967, 1968, 1980).

Any discussion of the grieving process must touch on Freud's groundbreaking "Mourning and Melancholia" (1915). With wonderful clarity Freud contrasts normal and pathological processes:

> As we have seen, however [p. 250f.], melancholia contains something more than normal mourning. In melancholia the relation to the object is no simple one; it is complicated by the conflict due to ambivalence. This ambivalence is either constitutional, i.e., is an element of every love relation formed by this particular ego, or else it proceeds precisely from those experiences that involved a threat of losing the object. For this reason the exciting causes of melancholia have a much wider range than those of mourning, which is for the most part occasioned only by a real loss of the object, by its death. In melancholia, accordingly, countless separate struggles are carried on over the object, in which hate and love contend with each other; the one seeks to detach the libido from the object, the other to maintain this position of the libido against the assault [p. 256].

Thus Freud explicitly mentions ambivalence as complicating loss. He also refers directly to "self-criticism" (p. 246) in a way that he would probably later call "guilt," once he had developed his conception of the role of the superego. But Freud quite clearly excludes shame:

> Finally, it must strike us that after all the melancholic does not behave in quite the same way as a person who is crushed by remorse and self-reproach in a normal fashion. Feelings of shame

in front of other people, which would more than anything characterize this latter condition, are lacking in the melancholic, or at least they are not prominent in him. One might emphasize the presence in him of an almost opposite trait of insistent communicativeness which finds satisfaction in self-exposure [p. 247].

Further on, Freud is even more explicit, privileging anger-related emotions as the prime complications of grieving, and excluding shame:

They are not ashamed and do not hide themselves, since everything derogatory that they say about themselves is at bottom said about someone else. Moreover, they are far from evincing toward those around them the attitude of humility and submissiveness that would alone befit such worthless people. On the contrary, they make the greatest nuisance of themselves, and always seem as though they felt slighted and had been treated with great injustice. All this is possible only because the reactions expressed in their behavior still proceed from a mental constellation of revolt, which has then, by a certain process, passed over into the crushed state of melancholia [p. 248].

Elsewhere (Buechler, 1995a) I have suggested that the subsequent interpersonal psychoanalytic literature on depression can be grouped according to whether anger or sadness is seen as central. Regardless, it is striking to me that psychoanalytic views generally parallel the emotion theory perspective (Izard, 1971, 1972, 1977), which is derived from research on the facial expression of emotions in normal populations. Despite their great differences in source material both views contrast simple grief (where one emotion predominates) with more complex depression (where several emotions combine).

The difference between normal loss reactions and pathological grief is so poetically described by Arieti (1978) that I will quote him at length:

Common is the sorrow that visits the human being when an adverse event hits his precarious existence or when the discrepancy between the way life is and the way it possibly could be becomes the center of his fervid reflection. In some people this sorrow comes and goes repeatedly, and in some others, only from time to time. It is painful, delays actions, and generally heals, often but not always after deepening its host's understanding and hastening his maturation.

Less common—but frequent enough to constitute major psychiatric concern—is the sorrow that does not abate with the passage of time, that seems exaggerated in relation to the supposed precipitating event, or inappropriate, or unrelated to any discernible cause, or replacing a more congruous emotion. This sorrow slows down, interrupts, or disrupts one's actions; it spreads a sense of anguish which may become difficult to contain; at times it tends to expand relentlessly into a psyche which seems endless in its capacity to experience mental pain; often it recurs even after appearing to be healed. This emotional state is generally called depression [p. 3].

We all suffer losses, and they bring us sorrow. I suggest that the sorrow itself is often the least helpful focus, in treatment. It is frequently more fruitful to explore the feelings that complicate the sorrow and the absence of other feelings that could modulate it. The overall topic of emotional balance is addressed in chapter 6. Here I focus specifically on the regret, loneliness, shame and despair that I believe can make loss unbearable. Other feelings, if present, may diminish the pain of loss. I believe that in the usual course of treatment, most especially at termination, we have opportunities to manifest and nurture what it emotionally takes to bear loss.

Wild with All Regret

Dear as remembered kisses after death,
And sweet as those by hopeless fancy feigned
On lips that are for others; deep as love
Deep as first love, and wild with all regret;
O Death in life, the days that are no more!

—Alfred Lord Tennyson,
"Tears, Idle Tears"

While Freud privileged anger-related emotions as complicating loss I believe regret plays a central role. Could Lear have borne the loss of Cordelia if he had less of his own folly to regret? More generally, can we find the strength to cope with sorrow when we have done all we can to minimize regret?

Grieving encumbered by regret is memorably portrayed in Terrence Rattigan's (1985) poignant play *In Praise of Love*.

Lydia, a survivor of early life war-related horrors, is married to Sebastian, a seemingly self-absorbed scholar, and they have one grown son. The play centers on the efforts of Lydia and Sebastian to help each other with the painful knowledge that Lydia is dying of a progressive disease that is related to her earlier malnutrition. A mutual friend of the couple, Mark, also tries to ease the general pain. Should Lydia and Sebastian speak directly about what is happening? How much can each do for the other? What might mitigate their suffering? Sebastian, undemonstrative, seemingly cocooned in his highly intellectual self-absorption, tells his friend Mark (p. 245):

	You see the thing is, Mark—the *un*-crying, unsentimental, un-self-pitying thing is that I didn't begin really to love her until I knew I was losing her.
Mark:	*(Not indulging him)* Yeh. That happens.
Sebastian:	Perhaps more to people like me than to people like you. You've always loved her, haven't you?
Mark:	I guess so.
Sebastian:	While I—I've only had about six months. Anybody but me would have started twenty-eight years sooner.

Just a bit later Sebastian explains (p. 247):

> *(Angrily)* Do you know what "le vice Anglais?"—the English vice—really is? Not flagellation, not pederasty—whatever the French believe it to be. It's our refusal to admit to our emotions. We think they demean us, I suppose.

> *(He covers his face)* Well I'm being punished now, all right—for a lifetime of vice. Very moral endings to a Victorian novel. I'm becoming maudlin. But, oh Mark, life without Lydia will be such unending misery.

But Rattigan allows his characters comfort at the end. Sebastian moves emotionally closer to their son, releasing Lydia from having to psychologically take care of everyone. Perhaps Lydia can just bear her own dying now that she needn't feel she is leaving Sebastian helpless. And perhaps Sebastian can just bear his loss now that he knows he did what he could to ease Lydia's way. Sebastian and Lydia modulate the unbearable for each other and themselves. Their loss is enormous. But perhaps if their loss is not joined with too profound regret it can—just— be borne.

Lonely Mourning

In one respect Freudian theory can lead the clinician away from being able to modulate sorrow helpfully. Freud believed that mourning is accomplished by remembering, and thereby letting go, of aspects of the lost object. I feel that this perspective, when applied clinically, might increase the patient's loneliness, exacerbating rather than ameliorating sorrow. That is, Freud would say that when someone dies we do some of the work of mourning at the next Thanksgiving, remembering just how he used to carve the turkey. For Freud remembering this detail is in the service of letting go of a "piece" of the object. But if continuity with the lost object, to avoid any unnecessary loneliness, is a crucial part of bearing loss, then the richly detailed memory should be used to *maintain* the tie to the inner object. Remembering just how he carved the turkey particularizes our picture of him. He feels nearer when we remember him with such specificity. Similarly, to honor the victims of atrocities we hold on to details of their suffering that make the victims remain palpable, ongoing presences. In this light the dissociation of the traumatized, a defensive effort to avoid those very vivid details that would bring painful memories to life, may actually exacerbate the loneliness of their sorrow. Their losses are compounded by the loss of connection to their own memories.

Gaines (1997) emphasized the importance of retaining rather than relinquishing inner objects in order to bear loss. Many religious and cultural rituals around death serve to delimit loneliness so we can face sorrow. Thus two antidotes to loneliness are potentially available to the mourner: maintenance of the inner object tie and the external presence of others. In Gaines's terms,

> The availability of other people with whom to share the connection to the lost object helps mourners to bring the relationship into the present context, making it part of their

shared ongoing lives. In a very important way, inner construction of objects draws on shared social construction of those objects [p. 559].

Elsewhere (Buechler, 2000) I have argued that the specificity of memories of the lost object is helpful in the grieving process. Here I suggest that this is because of the amelioration of loneliness that could otherwise complicate grief.

The Shame of Shame

It comes as no surprise that, as noted earlier, the classical view discounts the significance of shame as a complication of mourning. Clinicians have a long history of privileging other emotions over shame (O'Leary, 1988). No attempt to summarize that history will be made here, except for brief mention of two possible reasons for it:

1. Our countertransference to shame may be more intensely negative than to other emotions that are less identified with narcissism.
2. Shame, of all the emotions, is the only one regularly exacerbated by calling attention to it. Given our allegiance to heightening awareness, as clinicians, this may make us uneasy treating shame.

For these and probably many other reasons, I feel we are often content to ignore shame, in our patients and in ourselves. Thus we might easily fall in line with Freud's exclusion of shame from the list of emotions that complicate grief.

In a talk that counters this tendency, Bose (personal communication, February 2000) spoke of the struggle to create a coherent form for the sense of self. A patient of Bose's described the process. Speaking of herself, the patient said, "I realized that I can't separate myself from her, from the life of my childhood. I felt as a whole. As I was sitting there, this feeling of being constructed came over me—the feeling that I am put together, brick by brick, or pebble by pebble, that I was a being made into a very specific form."

Extending this thought, we can see how loss could create a shame that complicates sorrow. Loss means disruption in an ongoing connection (at least with the external object). The loss is not just of the other, it is *of the self in relation to that other*. For example, a patient's father died.

With this death the patient lost his sometimes-friend, sometimes-competitor, sometimes-ideal, and so on. He also lost the part of himself striving to impress his father. Of course, this is only true in a very limited external sense, but as a form, as a gestalt, he will know himself differently. He will not wake up next Sunday wondering if his dad will be proud of his golf prowess, as they shoot the seventh hole that day.

Relative impoverishment of the self is what shame is all about (O'Leary, 1988; O'Leary and Wright, 1986). Clinically I have found that a loss that frequently leads to ashamed depression is the loss not of a person, but of a possibility. Perhaps this is the hardest loss to forgive oneself for. Of course losses can coexist, so that a death may shock us into awareness of missed possibilities. A parent dies suddenly, precluding any chance of reconciliation with his adolescent daughter. The daughter mourns not just the loss of her father but the lost opportunity to become someone who could relate to him differently. In this loss sadness marries guilt, regret, and shame, and loneliness lurks, not far behind. The loss of the father is surely painful but the lost opportunity is a more complex loss, causing shame and therefore directly affecting the sense of self. When there is no refuge, when the world *and* the self become impoverished, the will to live can be sapped.

The middle-aged woman who recognizes, too late, that she will miss the joys of being a parent can feel acute pain over this lost opportunity. I think this often leads to depression because, although she may be very sad, she is not just sad. She may also feel ashamed that others were able to work out enjoying this experience, and she was not. Regret and even a kind of guilt toward the self can add to the pain. Again, loneliness is a frequent accompaniment. In this kind of loss the inner and outer worlds feel equally impoverished. There is no escape from pain; on top of an external loss there are intense negative feelings toward the self.

A woman in her mid-60s has recently lost both parents and her husband. Her mother finally succumbed to the Alzheimer's disease that had rendered her infantile and impossible to care for. Her father also died a gradual death, but with full mental faculties, outraged at the indignities of nursing-home life. Her husband's death was comparatively merciful, in that he didn't suffer much. But they had a long, harmonious marriage, and the loss of her life's companion was excruciating. The patient's question to me was unencumbered by theory or abstract philosophy. She asked how she could bear all the pain.

Do I, as an analyst, know anything that can really help this woman? What I believe is that nothing can decrease her enormous sadness. She should be sad, and it would be absurd to try to "cure" her of it. My contribution might lie in helping her with *how* to be sad, or how to be *just* sad.

In this case, self-reproach severely complicates the patient's emotional life. She feels she has failed everyone. She is never attentive enough to satisfy her own standards. Similarly, each of her adult children fails to pass muster. For this patient the sense of shame over being inadequate as a daughter, wife, and mother is enormous. Guilt vies with shame in intensity. That is, the patient feels she is at fault for having neglected everyone (guilt) and has been an ill-equipped, sorry failure in every role (shame). Thus there is no comfort for her. She has lost the (external) objects *and* the sense of self that made her life rich enough to enjoy. I can do nothing about the external losses. Her sorrow at how each loved one died seems understandable and inevitable. But the patient has "lost" herself along with her parents and husband, and this truncated self-esteem may not be immutable.

We often help people bear loss by having a different focus from the patient's. Treatment cannot and should not try to deal with everything. The pain inherent in living life is not amenable to treatment. Life hurts. As analysts we can do nothing to change that. But we enable people to bear this pain when we focus on the other emotions they also feel.

I believe that shame often shadows sorrow. As is its nature, it hides its face, blending in with the pain of the loss of a loved one. When we lose someone significant, the world is never the same. Neither are we.

When the Wreck Has Been

People often make no secret of the despair that can accompany mourning. Although despair generally announces itself, it can't always reflect on itself. Perhaps Joyce Carol Oates (1993) put this most succinctly when she said that true despair is as "unreflective as flesh lacking consciousness" (p. 3). Oates also quoted Emily Dickinson's wonderful analogy:

> The difference between Despair
> And Fear—is like the One
> Between the instant of a Wreck—
> And when the Wreck has been—
>
> The Mind is smooth—no Motion—
> Contented as the Eye
> Upon the Forehead of a Bust—
> That knows—it cannot see—

In *Despair and the Return of Hope,* Shabad (2001) refers to the "unused life" as a cause of despair (p. 282). Despair brings time into the equation, in the sense that it expresses the feeling that things will never change for the better.

For this reason, ameliorative efforts often introduce the idea that the pain will be time-limited. Perhaps without thinking in emotion theory terms, they rely on countering the despairing belief that pain will be unending. When that despair is dispelled, the rest of the pain often can be borne. William Styron, who wrote of his own battles against despair (2002), expressed this succinctly:

It is of great importance that those who are suffering a siege, perhaps for the first time, be told—be convinced, rather—that the illness will run its course and that they will pull through. A tough job, this, calling "Chin up!" from the safety of the shore to a drowning person is tantamount to insult, but it has been shown over and over again that if the encouragement is dogged enough—and the support equally committed and passionate—the endangered one can nearly always be saved. Most people in the grip of depression at its ghastliest are, for whatever reason, in the state of unrealistic hopelessness, torn by exaggerated ills and fatal threats that bear no resemblance to actuality. It may require on the part of friends, lovers, family, admirers, an almost religious devotion to persuade the sufferers of life's worth, which is so often in conflict with a sense of their own worthlessness, but such devotion has prevented countless suicides [p. 122].

I came upon my own interest in despairing responses to loss through the study of burnout in analysts (Buechler, 1992, 2000).

Briefly, I believe burnout is a response to a loss of faith in the profession. The burned-out analyst can no longer believe in the worth of his chosen field. The losses at the heart of burnout are cumulative and may include lost expectations for career advancement, literal losses of patients and income, losses of pride because of a demoralizing climate for mental health care, lost hopes in the treatment of particular patients, lost stamina due to the work's stresses and rigors, and lost feelings of integrity, because of having to continue going through the motions of treating patients, for economic reasons. Of course, underlying character issues in the individual analyst are also involved. But there are aspects of our work, most especially its injunction to endure all our losses with silent stoicism, that I think are conducive to burnout. Despair can grow with the understanding that the losses will never end, that we will eventually lose every treatment partner we engage.

I believe that the burnout that is a despairing response to cumulative loss can take subtle forms. Sometimes, I feel, making the work matter less can be used defensively. For example, I think that believing analysis is "dead" or "about to die" can provide some with an illusory sense that one's own disappointments don't matter and should not be taken personally. Of course this doesn't work. The burned-out analyst has suffered the greatest possible loss in losing faith in the worth of his professional talents.

To return to Dickinson's poem, in despair the wreck has been and so need no longer be feared. This seems to promise peace, an end to the struggle against loss. But at what price!

The Well-Borne Loss

The central issue in mental health is the ability to deal with losses. Each person's life is full of major and minor losses and mourning reactions. Those who cope well can again become integrated; those who have difficulties will develop emotional or physical problems [Krupp and Krupp, 1980, p. 633].

What makes loss bearable? By now, I hope it is clear that one answer for me is that loss is more bearable the more it is *just* loss, relatively uncomplicated by regret, shame, loneliness, and endless despair. Of course I do not privilege these emotions and ignore the anger- and guilt-based affects that have received more analytic attention.

We know that even loss that is "just" loss can be extremely painful. Like Sullivan (1953), however, I have faith that human beings have remarkable powers to cope with life, if defensive obstacles can be recognized and modified. Facilitating that process is the job of the analyst. Like all other important changes this doesn't usually come about during the session. Treatment in general, and insight in particular, on its own, is usually not powerful enough to profoundly change people. Life experience changes people. But treatment can help make that experience possible, and be, in itself, a "laboratory" for developing the strength to bear loss. With grievous loss, part of the task is recognition of the inevitable sadness of being human.

Only Connect

Thus the well-borne loss is possible in the context where interpersonal support is available, if needed; the inevitable sadness is not pathologized, and other, complicating emotions are addressed. Sadness treated as a part of life can bring us more firmly to each other, in the shared human condition, and bid us savor joyful moments.

Unholy Ghost (Casey, 2001), a book of short essays, each by a writer who has intimately known loss, suggests the kinds of human contact that sometimes help alleviate its pain. The touch of a friend, the song of a child, the devotion of a helper or advocate can make a difference. A passage from this book (Manning, 2001) poignantly captures how this can come about:

> At the very end, I kept going only for my daughter. Every morning, Keara stumbles semiconscious into the bathroom and turns on the shower. Within the space of 30 seconds she starts to sing. She starts out humming so softly that her voice blends with the spray as it bounces off the wall. And then she chooses her song—sometimes sweet and lyrical, sometimes loud and rocking. Each morning, when I had to face another day on two hours of sleep and absolutely no hope, I leaned against the bathroom door waiting for her to sing and let her voice invite me to try for one more day [p. 266].

I feel that these words express the essence of our therapeutic task, which is to address the overall balance of emotions (see chapter 6).

I imagine Manning hears, in her child's song, that something having nothing to do with loss also exists. Keara's un–self-conscious daily progress from soft hum to song is unfazed by Manning's depression. It is separate enough to have a life of its own. It doesn't contradict Manning's pain. Instead it exists alongside pain. The swelling song is also part of reality. Life goes on. It seems to me that what helps Manning is the feeling that, in addition to her helpless depression, youthful exuberance also still exists. Sadness is still very real but not overpowering side by side with the joy of listening to the sound of her daughter's vitality.

Fond Memories

> I don't miss Iris. Perhaps because I don't "remember" her. Not in the way I remember things and people in the past, who are truly gone. No wonder she didn't want a memorial service. She knew I would not need to remember her in that way.
>
> When we left home in former times, before Iris became ill, she was always there to look after me. She enjoyed getting the tickets at the train station, paying the taxi, steering me through the caverns of the Underground. She kept me safe. And she will still do that at home, the place where in those days I used to look after her.
>
> I sleep quietly now, with Iris quiet beside me. I drop off in the daytime, too, and wake up feeling calm and cheerful, as if Iris were there. But one morning recently I caught the tail of my vest on our Windsor chair and spilled my mug of tea. I wanted to tell Iris about it, but when I got upstairs I found that she was not there and I couldn't tell her [Bayley, 1999a, p. 43].

Bayley's remarkable work tells the story of his marriage to Iris Murdoch, philosopher and fiction writer, who died of Alzheimer's disease. Through most of her last years Bayley cared for her at home. His struggle to find the strength for this task is movingly portrayed in this short piece, "Last Jokes," and in the longer versions, *An Elegy for Iris* (1999b) and *Iris and Her Friends: A Memoir of Memory and Desire* (2000). But what do we, as psychoanalysts, make of Bayley's statement that he doesn't miss Iris as he would miss someone truly gone? Is this a form of denial, or an expression of the kind of continuity with the inner object described by Gaines (1997)? Should we promote this kind of thinking?

I suggest that Bayley can bear Iris's death because he has lost *only* her physical presence. That hurts (perhaps especially when he wants to tell her something), but it can be borne. Because of what Bayley *doesn't* feel, he can bear the pain of the loss. He doesn't seem to feel that psychological health would mean separating himself from Iris and spending less time with her now. He sleeps "quietly," "calm and cheerful." The soothing sense of being joined to such a remarkable, beloved woman brings Bayley peace. His peace may stem, partially, from knowing he gave Iris the best death she could have.

What can we do for each other at the end of life? How much should denial be a part of our relationship with death? Is it essential for the person who is dying, or for those who love them, or for neither? How much can we prepare ourselves, and each other, for this part of life? These questions are taken up in Terence Rattigan's poignant play, *In Praise of Love,* discussed earlier. There, too, a case is made for the human need to soften loss by limiting the pain to only sadness, as much as possible; adding human connections, made newly possible by a greater awareness of vulnerability; and keeping alive the relationship to the "lost" one.

The Treatment Microcosm

Fortunately, analytic treatment affords numerous opportunities to the analyst to deal with loss. There are obvious examples of this, such as the way the analyst deals with actual separations. Analysts differ considerably in how we handle vacations and other time gaps. We make statements about who we are and how we believe in living life every time we deal with a missed appointment. I am not just referring to our overt behaviors (e.g., whether to try to make up lost appointments, whether to charge), but also the textural feel of our attitude. What, for example, is my particular way of bearing the fact that all treatment relationships inevitably end? How do I manifest my personal balance of emotional reactions to the loss? Do I make occasional reference to termination, avoid it, or bring it up every chance I can? Do I seem to be trying to master anxiety about it? Do I treat termination as an indictment of *my* work or as an achievement of *our* work? Am I anxious about the loss of income, and is my anxiety palpable? What is the spirit I bring to this issue? Do I seem to have more hope than sadness about it?

Similarly when I have to miss a session how hard do I try to make it up? What does this say to the patient about who I am and the balance of emotions I feel about the separation? How hard do I work to create continuity by, for example, making reference to previous sessions? Is that part of how I deal with gaps of time?

We put our personal stamp on how we deal with treatment's microcosm of life. Like the rest of life, treatment is finite. It involves two people attempting to cope with the paradox of being related yet separate. I show the patient how I handle manifestations of all these issues in the way I work. Inevitably, in coping with the treatment relationship I am also demonstrating a particular balance of emotions. I hope, for example, to convey how my real curiosity and wish to be of help outweigh concerns about how intelligent my inquiry makes me look.

Perhaps, as in other relationships, in treatment it is at least as significant who we are not, as who we are (Buechler, 2002c). I think it is important not to be someone who can't openly address separation. For example, a supervisee recounted the ending of a fairly involved treatment. He became preoccupied with why the patient was terminating. Reasons had been offered, but they didn't seem compelling.

Listening, I was very aware of something missing. This had been the kind of treatment that really helps an emotionally adolescent patient grow up. The patient had had a painful, extraordinarily lonely childhood with undemonstrative parents and many siblings fighting for attention. The treatment helped him find a good career and experiment in ultimately untenable, but enjoyable romantic relationships. For no reason persuasive to the analyst or his supervisor, the patient had decided to terminate the treatment.

I noted that, if the patient quit now, neither participant would have expressed what the work meant to him. For me it was as though both were avoiding the pain of the loss, by not talking about the meaning of the relationship. My comment led to a fuller engagement, although some mystery about the ending of the work remained. In my view the analyst must not be someone who avoids facing the full extent of the pain of loss. She must also be someone who avoids pathologizing the normal pain of living life. She must be able to see, as the poet William Blake wrote, a world in a grain of sand. A microcosm (like treatment) offers an opportunity to deal with some of life's major challenges together. We grapple with issues of interpersonal trust, dependence, and commitment, personal inadequacy, failure, disappointed hope, the past that is remembered and the past that is forgotten, power and control, the limits of time, the shame of "slips," and the finality of endings, to name a few. Like a death the end of treatment means the end of contact, although, unlike death, termination is not unalterable. The analyst must be someone who faces endings squarely, who looks them in the eye. We mustn't (obsessionally) try to use words to paper over the pain. We mustn't avoid the reality of the personal loss (Coltart, 1993; Buechler, 2000).

Analysts often try to make light of the incredible number of losses we bear, acting as though we can "move on" to the next patient when the buzzer sounds, like some kind of Pavlovian caricature. We may sometimes pretend (to ourselves) that patients are replaceable. Of course we know that isn't so, but I think we still have difficulty admitting what patients mean to us personally. Facing the meaning of the relationship and, therefore, the meaning of its termination is one of the challenges of being an analyst. For us, as for anyone, it is a matter of balance. Acknowledging the inherent sadness is an important first step. This sadness will be more bearable if it is unaccompanied by great shame, guilt, unresolved anger, loneliness, regret, despair.

Many passages in treatment, but, most especially, its ending, give us chances to live out loud, in front of the patient. In how we approach these junctures we make palpable what we believe is meaningful about our work and the rest of our lives. In bearing loss we have to call on all our resources as human beings. We rely on our faith in the value of our effort to give us balance. We keep the memory of our patients alive by reflecting on our experiences with them. Like John Bayley we bear loss by losing only the person's physical presence.

A Job for Sadness

I would like to end this chapter with the story of a patient of my own, who died in her 30s, after over a decade of treatment. We were, at the time, making real progress toward the patient becoming truly able to enter a relationship. Her life had been encumbered by physical disabilities. She struggled courageously to surmount these obstacles. Now it looked like she would emerge from her psychological constraints, as well. Her sudden death, over a weekend, was completely unexpected.

I have struggled with my own shock and pain about her death for years. In some ways I felt the timing could not have been worse. "Not now," I remember feeling. Just when so much seemed possible. And yet, I was also grateful we came as far as we did.

I wrote about these feelings in a previous paper (Buechler, 2000). There (p. 89) I tried to express how this loss has affected me. Because I have no other way to put it, I would like to repeat what I said has changed, over time, in my experience of this loss, and what, I expect, will never change.

> The pain of her loss is no less now than it was when she died, and my feelings of regret that she didn't have more time are unchanged. What is different is that years of self-reflection have clarified some of the personal meanings of her life and death to me. Now I bring this greater clarity to each instance of actively mourning her loss. And cumulative experience has taught me something about how much she contributed to my personal and professional growth. Every current clinical and nonclinical moment that the experience of her illuminates increases my appreciation of her. Every time remembering her helps me in some way, the balance of what I gained from her versus what I suffered changes. I know much more now about what seeing her did, and still does, for me professionally and personally, and how I would like to use that growth. The sadness is doing its essential job, of binding me more firmly to life.

8 *Developing Integrity*

But yield who will to their separation,
My object in living is to unite
My avocation and my vocation
As my two eyes make one in sight.
Only where love and need are one,
And the work is play for mortal stakes,
Is the deed ever really done
For heaven and the future's sakes.

Robert Frost,
"Two Tramps in Mud Time"

Frost is describing a self-cohesion that may sound foreign to our postmodern ears, accustomed to multiple self-states as normal (Bromberg, 1998). Is treatment an exercise in recognizing inner diversity (of me–you patterns, Sullivan, 1953; of personalities, Levenson, 1991; of selves, Mitchell, 1993) or finding inner cohesion? Is inner cohesion an outlived, old-fashioned virtue? Is it, as Cushman and Gilford (1999) suggest, seen as a liability in today's world, which has shifted from valuing

a self with a deep, potentially rich interior, to a self with a greatly attenuated or shallow interior space; from a self that had

a wish for what Foucault called a "richly furnished interior," to
a self with a need for many varied exteriors that one can quickly
select from and present to the world; from a self that should be
singular and unified, to a self that should be multiple and
decentered . . . from a self that hoped to be fundamentally trans-
formed to a self that hopes to present the most effective and attractive identity at the most propitious moment . . . to be more
alluring, effective, and elusive . . . solidity, courage, self-knowledge, and self-respect seem less like a virtue than a recipe for
self-destruction [pp. 18–19].

What can the term *integrity* mean to us now?

Years before my analytic candidacy I was in treatment with a respected, traditionally trained analyst. Her physical deformity spoke
volumes about the trials she had personally endured. Although not
particularly self-revealing, she was very clear about the necessity to
meet life with courage. It would have been hard for me to look at her
and say that I was unable to face up to the challenges of my own life.
When she tried to enlist my courage, I didn't feel she was asking any
more of me than she expected of herself.

Her words and her personal conduct seemed to me to have a resonance that I feel expresses a form of integrity. The dictionary (*American
Heritage, New College Edition,* 1969) offers us an evocative array of meanings for integrity. Among them is "moral soundness, especially as it is
revealed in dealings that test steadfastness to truth, purpose, responsibility or trust." Another meaning is "the state of being unimpaired;
soundness; completeness; unity." I believe that words and actions that
match can have a powerful impact. When an open and direct person
advises us to be open and direct and manifests these qualities in the
way he advocates them, he gets our attention. In treatment, in supervision, in teaching, presenting and writing when the medium resonates
with the message we are more likely to be inspired. The "unity" or "unimpaired" quality is in the adherence to the same code in word and
deed. In Frost's language, we might say that in integrity our motives
and our actions form a seamless, centered whole. Love, need, work,
and play get their resonance from having in common that they are directed toward "heaven and the future's sakes."

In contrast when we ask people to do as we say, not as we do, I think
we turn peoples' attention toward this discrepancy. We more often

transfix than transform. We strike them dumb, arrest progress as they struggle to make sense out of mystification.

This chapter addresses integrity for the analytic candidate, the clinician in private practice, and the supervisor-teacher-speaker-author. Each of these contexts provides a set of challenges to integrity.

Integrity in Training: If It's Tuesday, I Must Be Interpersonal

A candidate, a woman with a great deal of professional experience who has decided to further her treatment career by being trained analytically, arrives for supervision with me. She is visibly uneasy, trying to contain anxiety, fear of shame, and anger. She feels reduced to her eight-year-old self, with her hand firmly planted in the cookie jar. Self-editing every word, she nevertheless tries to tell me the awful truth.

After much hesitation, she intimates that it bothers her a great deal that I don't seem to ascribe to the same school of thought as her other supervisor. I feel she is disappointed in me. She wanted to believe in me. Now she can't. She wanted to use me as *the* model (not *a* model) who would give her hope that she, too, could become an analyst. Now she isn't sure. What if my point of view is wrong?

Because it isn't always noticed, I want to emphasize the loneliness inherent in the candidate's position. Loneliness can be differentiated from aloneness in that in loneliness we feel a painful, unremediable sense of loss (Fromm-Reichmann, 1959). In loneliness there may be no hope of ever being understood (Buechler, 1998). This can be true for the candidate, as she discovers she is the only one on earth in exactly her position. How can she split herself, learning and practicing different methods, in various supervisions, and still retain any semblance of a sense of integrity? Will the feeling of wholeness be restored to her on graduation day? Is this confusion really temporary? Will she *ever* have conviction about what she is doing clinically?

How will I react if she tells me her other supervisor recommended a holding, empathic stance that seems to work better than anything I've suggested? She committed the sin of trying out this stance with "our" patient! Hence, the hand-in-the-cookie-jar feeling.

Loneliness can be contagious. In this supervision, *I* am beginning to feel unalterably alone, misunderstood, and pinned down like a collected butterfly. I have been classified according to my "species" of analysis. I am now a representative of a type. That's all I'm allowed to be in this supervision. I am expected to keep anything that doesn't fit this categorization to myself. Even if I try to escape, by voicing eclecticism, it may not be recognized. Hence I feel permanently alone with much of my own sense of my clinical stance.

What If the Center Cannot Hold?

Learning to conduct any psychological treatment but especially psychoanalysis is a real challenge to the feeling of integrity. In a paper on the supervision of candidates treating "borderline" patients (Buechler, 1996), I described the fractured position of the candidate, who is often pulled in one direction by the patient (toward frame breaking, advice giving) and in the other direction by the supervisor (toward analytic neutrality and abstinence). If we suppose the candidate to be someone who likes to please people, this can be a troubling experience. Trying to please the patient (or at least not lose him) the candidate does a lot of bending (bends over backward, bends the frame). Then comes the hour for supervision. Wanting to avoid displeasing the supervisor, should she "fudge" and fail to mention some of the bending? Should she assume the stance that pleases the patient in the treatment, and the stance that pleases the supervisor in supervision? What if there are several supervisors? Where is the candidate's integrity?

We can already see some of the many challenges to the experience of wholeness that this situation poses. I would add a peculiar sense many candidates have: that they have to jettison prior professional personas to don the cloak of the naïve student. For (at least) four years they are no longer professors, experienced therapists, and so on. They are novices. It is true that in terms of doing analysis candidates are generally inexperienced. Most often, however, they come into training with rich backgrounds of other forms of expertise and life experience. Where does the injunction to jettison these identities come from? How can the candidate ignore such significant aspects of his established self and still retain a sense of personal wholeness and integrity?

I suggest that, depending on his character, the candidate in this fragmenting situation may unconsciously try to resort to anger to maintain cohesion. Anger allows us to gather ourselves together, to mobilize and reenter the fray. In battle we don't focus on pleasing disparate factions. Aside from this functional use, anger may be a response to the disappointment of lost illusions. We often come into mental health professions expecting our faculty members to conduct their personal and professional lives with more wisdom than it turns out to be realistic to expect.

Anger can be focused on an aspect of the training, such as the courses, or particular faculty members, or classmates, or oneself. I believe that this last alternative, anger directed inward, often takes the form of a helpless confusion. The candidate appears uncomfortable, halting, frozen, silent, or emotionally overwhelmed. Signs of obsessional defensiveness, such as excess wordiness, indirectness, self-editing, passive-aggressive behavior, intellectualization, and compartmentalization are common. This anger directed toward the self does not provide the sought cohesion but, rather exacerbates fragmentation.

Don't Look Behind That Curtain

Challenges to feeling a sense of integrity, acting with integrity, and being perceived as having integrity don't end on graduation day. In a sense training serves as a forewarning of life as a clinician, wherein there are countless challenges to the inner experience and outward appearance of integrity. Managed care, in our bottom-line–driven culture, requires us to communicate information that is often, at best, distorted by omission. Dealing with insurance we have countless opportunities to worry about the state of health of our own integrity. If I report all I believe to be true (including, perhaps, that I think the work with this patient will probably take at least five years, at three times per week, etc.), will I lose needed coverage for the patient? If so I may have the pleasure of believing I have maintained my integrity, but at the expense (literally) of the patient! Do I give a patient a diagnosis that, although accurate to my mind, will be costly (not reimbursed) or potentially dangerous (to his position, if somehow disclosed)?

In all these situations the threat to a sense of integrity stems from the clinician being unable to be her whole self. Our literature is replete with conceptualizations of the meaning of multiple selves (see Cushman, 1995, for a penetrating analysis of Kohut's views on the concept of "self"), but I believe we still await clarity about whether to view it as a naturally occurring, benign state (e.g., Sullivan's, 1953, me–you patterns); as a naturally occurring, sometimes problematic state (Bromberg, 1998); or as a form of pathology (Kernberg, 1980).

In Sullivan's view (1953, 1954, 1956), we have varying personalities adapted to differing interpersonal contexts. This is a necessary, and actually beneficial, situation. More recently Mitchell (1993) posited a similar thesis. He believed we must learn to tolerate experiencing multiple versions of self and still retain a sense of "continuity" that I would say is his way of describing integrity:

> One of the great benefits of the analytic process is that the more the analysand can tolerate experiencing multiple versions of himself, the stronger, more resilient, and more durable he experiences himself to be. Conversely, the more the analysand can find continuities across his various experiences, the more he can tolerate the identity diffusion entailed by containing multiple versions of self. The analyst helps to enable him to find and recognize himself when he is experiencing and behaving "out of character," and it is that recognition that opens up the possibility of a more complex, richer experience [p. 116].

Thus for Mitchell the sense of wholeness should, ideally, persist along with a healthy diversity of selves. Although Winnicott (1960) and Guntrip (1969) also expect more than one organized self, they see the opposition of false and true self as an ordinary, but nonetheless undesirable, state that should be treated: "The 'true self in cold storage' could, it seems to me, mean either the repressed regressed ego or the dissociated unevoked psychic potential. In both cases the patient has lost touch with his own potentialities, and we have to help him find himself" (Guntrip, 1969, p. 253).

Even more explicitly viewing multiple self-states as pathology Kernberg (1975) notes the following:

> The normal integrated self and its related integrated conceptions of others (integrated object representations) guarantee a sense of continuity throughout time and under varying circumstances. They also guarantee a sense of belonging to a network of human relations that makes life meaningful, and they guarantee the ordinary "self-feeling" we take for granted and which

is normally only threatened by the most extreme and unusual psychosocial traumata or life-threatening situations [p. 213].

Considerations of whether multiple self-states are benign, frequent and potentially problematic, or serious pathology apply equally to clinicians and their patients. I believe we cannot define integrity without taking a position on the issue of the normality of varying self-states.

Levenson (1991) warns us against mixing our metaphors. In his language, we should be aware of when we are working with the concept of character versus personality. Character implies a structure (p. 240), a construct, a thing, whereas personality is the sum of all one's recurrent interpersonal patterns. Thus with the more modern concept of personality we move toward greater comfort with multiple self-states.

So far I am mainly considering the *clinician's* sense of integrity, although these issues obviously also apply to the patient. I am suggesting that analysis constantly presents us with situations that test steadfastness to truth, purpose, responsibility, or trust and consequently they reveal our integrity, as described earlier in this chapter. To me, analytic integrity is the ability to bring one's whole self to the analytic task. Mind, heart, and spirit make the same commitment. It is more than just honesty, at least in the limited sense of truth telling. It speaks to motive and not just behavior. The patient should be able to count on the clinician's integrity. The resonance between my own analyst's statements and actions lent power to her impact on me.

What about normal self-state fluctuation, as understood by Mitchell (1993) among many other writers? Doesn't this apply to clinicians?

Although the goal of consistent self-presentation may not be achievable, I believe it is an important goal to uphold. In the following pages, I suggest how I think this applies to both patient and clinician.

Some analytic traditions especially highlight integrity in the analyst, as well as in the patient. It is my opinion that this is one of the legacies of the work of Erich Fromm. Similar views have been expressed by Biancoli (2002), Funk (2002), and Ortmeyer (2002). Although Fromm famously lacked neutral evenhandedness at times (Maccoby, 1996), his emphasis on integrity, and his own integrity, shone through (Roazen, 1996). Fromm's writing (1955, 1962, 1976) shed light on the "deals" we make to get by in our culture. Our stance toward these deals, inside and outside of the treatment, tells the patient a great deal about our standards for our own integrity.

One Hand Washing the Other

In a sense every relationship is a kind of deal. Expectations are excited, fulfilled to some degree, modified. The deals that compromise integrity are those that divide us against ourselves. They may be initiated by the patient or clinician and entered into freely or under constraint. What they have in common is that the deal requires sacrificing one aspect of oneself in favor of others. I illustrate this with examples where either the clinician or the patient (or both) feel compelled to abandon integrity, wholeness, intactness of self, to preserve some semblance of the relationship.

Selecting and Initiating Training Cases

Candidates in analytic training need a certain number of supervised patient hours to graduate. Even in predoctoral, nonanalytic programs, some clinical experience may be required. In analytic training the candidate has often put the rest of his adult life on hold while he finishes the program. He wants these credentials for many reasons, some practical, some having to do with pride, some with the desire to do the work he chose.

As an example, the candidate does an intake, a possible analytic patient. But that's not what the patient had in mind. She came for less intensive and more speedy help with her life. The question often becomes how to "educate her" to want analytic treatment. The fee for the more frequent analytic sessions is often lower than the psychotherapy fee. Hence the deal: she gets less expensive treatment but still tries, perhaps, to tailor its agenda to her own goals. The candidate fulfills a requirement but has to overlook the fact that the patient isn't a perfect training case. The various reasons for this can include her acting out potential, her diagnosis, the absence of self-reflective ability or interest, and her agenda for treatment.

In this scenario, very often, everyone does well. The patient gets careful, intensive, supervised treatment at a low cost. The candidate gets valuable experience and a notch closer to qualifying in his profession. It is fine, in many senses. I am not suggesting that there is anything improper, unethical, or unhelpful about it for all concerned. From my point of view, however, there is one major problem. How can we train candidates to expose bargains patients try to make if we also create pressure for the candidate and patient to make a deal?

A related problem is the issue of assessment of the patient's "analyzability" and diagnosis. In the past the custom was that patients were chosen to be training cases, based on their capacity for the work. Although this no doubt meant very different things to different evaluators, it *was* taken to mean *something*. Today, partially because training centers need analytic cases and partly because we have come to believe in applying analytic methods to a wider spectrum of patients, the concept of assessing analyzability has lost meaning. The assessment can be largely an empty exercise, a rubber stamp issued if the patient agrees to the terms (fee, schedule) of the deal. No one is getting cheated. But I believe there is a fundamental difficulty, in that this training cannot nurture the development of analytic integrity.

The supervisor is drawn in as well, pressured to "preside" over the deal. Each participant loses integrity in the sense of wholeness, unity. The patient must, at least temporarily, accept a regimen that can seem unrelated to some of her needs. Doing this requires a kind of privileging of part of what she wants over other parts. I see it as a fragmentation of her feelings and desires.

It is not so different for the other participants, the candidate and supervisor, who, I suggest, also must fragment. From Winnicott's (1960) or Guntrip's (1969) perspective, false self-accommodation is privileged over the expression of the "true self." In other words, we all go along to get along. But at what price?

Conducting Training Cases

Compromise doesn't end at intake. The candidate is often afraid to anger (lose) the patient, feeling this will negatively impact or at least retard his training. This means he can't adopt whatever therapeutic approach seems indicated. Certain skills, like the analysis of defense, become especially difficult to learn in this context. Pointing out defensive behavior inherently has the potential to be upsetting for almost all patients. For example, reflecting on obsessional language carries the danger that the patient may feel narcissistically injured by the interpretation.

In general, the learning of the timing of interpretations is problematic in this context, where the "customer" has to be kept "happy" enough to stay. This often evokes obsessional defensiveness in the candidate as well as the supervisor who need to control something they really can't control (whether the patient stays in treatment). This could evoke just about anybody's obsessional use of language, attempting, sometimes, to interpret in overly wordy or abstract terms to avoid offending. Thus, if the candidate does show obsessional tendencies it is not clear what this means about him, and hence it is not as useful as it could be, for his personal analysis and supervision. Also, optimal learning cannot possibly occur in the anxious state this inevitably creates. But, once again, it is the difficulty developing integrity I am emphasizing here. How can we expect the candidate to be forthright about whether the patient needs analytic treatment, is benefiting, is ready to terminate, should be confronted more, is misguided about the limits of the treatment relationship, or has unrealistic expectations, when the candidate has so much at stake in keeping the patient in treatment? How can the candidate attain true conviction about his style of treatment in this context? How can the candidate learn the freedom to interpret the patient's pressures for narcissistic gratification when he feels obliged to accede to them?

Conducting Private Treatment

As has already been noted, private practice abounds with challenges to the clinician's integrity—for example, from managed care and other insurance providers. A few other sources of difficulty maintaining integrity will be mentioned here.

Both participants may be reluctant to injure the self-esteem of the other. I believe there can be sound (noncollusive) reasons for holding one's tongue. But in a collusion, we refrain because something crucial is personally at stake, so we are not free to choose our response. We have lost the wholeness, unity that is integrity in that we have bartered our (in)sight. We are creating a façade of collaboration, but nothing is really happening.

An example would be the patient who comes to treatment complaining about a partner, unwilling to look at her own contribution to the problems. If we go along with this agenda to keep the patient in treatment, we have lost integrity. Whether the "other" is a parent, marital partner, child, or employer doesn't matter. To act as though the "other" is the whole problem is usually abandoning our own broader vision of the situation in order to placate the patient.

This often creates a treatment impasse because we can't really help someone who is not present. In this situation, no one is fully present. The clinician is dividing himself into the covert assessor of the patient's role in the problems and the overt assessor of the partner's role. This division complicates the treatment. How can we work on the patient's paranoid suspicions about what we "really" think and feel when we are hiding what we really think and feel? How can we work on the patient's schizoid false self when we are manifesting our own?

Treatment as Seduction

A direct articulation of the mutual seduction that creates many treatment stalemates might go something like this:

Patient: Can you help me get a better response from my environment, without really changing how I conduct myself?

Analyst: I'll play along with that goal for a while, hoping to get you to see you should want to change how you fundamentally operate. But I'm afraid to tell you this.

Patient: If you threaten how I function too much I'll leave treatment.

Analyst: [Remembering Freud's experience with Dora, for example] Losing a patient before there is a chance to analyze her interpersonal patterns is a bad outcome. I'll do whatever I have to do to keep you in the treatment. For now I'll put aside much of what I really think and feel. But I'll soon get impatient with this.

Patient: A deal is a deal. Whatever you seem willing to do initially commits you to that approach to my problems.

Levenson (1982) usefully argues for inclusion of the understanding of the goals of the treatment, as an aspect of the frame. Mitchell (1993) contrasts the "hopes" of the patient versus the "hopes" of the analyst. However we refer to it, we need to examine whether we are making promises we can't keep.

Other collusive temptations include treating the work as more similar to friendship than it truly is, being willing to just get through the hour and ignoring the transference so as to avoid something "messy." Every session is a challenge to find a way to live with integrity.

Wholeness

As has already been mentioned, candidates in training often feel required to jettison previous identities and attainments and become blank pages for teachers and supervisors to fill in. This, too, carries over past graduation. I have often consulted with trained clinicians who are reluctant to bring their experience as parents into their work. They seem to feel it's worse than irrelevant—it could be a contaminant! Would they feel the same way about their own experiences growing older, being adolescent, falling in love?

I am not arguing against analytic neutrality or for personal disclosure, but simply for bringing our whole awareness of what it means to be human into our work. Of course our personal experience is, by definition, subjective and, to some extent, unique. It shouldn't be imposed, as a standard or model. But it must not be sacrificed as a resource, or "played down" as unimportant, or even a liability. My experience is that most especially women who are mothers and train for a professional role seem to feel apologetic, as though being a mother brands them as nonintellectual, or nonanalytic, or professionally incompetent. I think this issue is important for many reasons, but here I am only discussing one—the loss of integrity, in the sense of unity and wholeness, in turning one's back on a significant aspect of oneself. It is a tremendous loss—of a rich reservoir of human experience, of dignity, self-respect, and integrity. We need to bring our whole self to work, because doing treatment takes everything we have to offer, and because if we sacrifice our own integrity, we can't help other people reclaim theirs.

On the other hand, bringing one's whole self to any human interchange can be a source of joy (Buechler, 2002b). In *The Sane Society,* Fromm (1955) passionately argues for wholeness:

> One cannot separate work activity from political activity, from the use of leisure time and from personal life. If work were to become interesting without the other spheres of life becoming human, no real change would occur. In fact, it could not become interesting. It is the very evil of present-day culture

that it separates and compartmentalizes the various spheres of living. The way to sanity lies in overcoming this split and in arriving at a new unification and integration within society and within the individual being [p. 326].

Many Hats, One Head

A wonderful aspect of analytic professional life is its diversity. Aside from the clinical work (which, obviously, has its own built-in diversity), teaching, supervising, writing, and presenting at conferences are available avenues for self-expression. I know many colleagues who agree with me that each of these activities cross-fertilizes the others. When I am writing something, it is with me in sessions with patients. I feel it makes my work richer, more interesting to me. It adds a dimension to everything else I do.

In a recent book on affect intolerance in the patient and the analyst, Stanley Coen (2002) writes about the importance of sharing our work with colleagues:

It is a psychoanalytic premise that we all have limitations in what we can tolerate, in ourselves and in others, limitations that blind us some of the time. Discussants and clinical authors, looking together, can see more than either can see alone. Even good treatments become stuck as the therapeutic couples lose their way. Presenting clinical work allows others to help a treating therapist to regain therapeutic perspective and see what is being enacted and has remained, however long, outside of the therapeutic couple's awareness [p. 182].

Coen himself provides an example of integrity, in the sense of wholeness. In a review of his book, I commented on this quality (Buechler, 2003). I noted that his Coen-ness in everything he does, challenges us to rethink the concept of integrity. Despite wearing many hats, Coen palpably remains Coen.

The sheer diversity of our roles (not to speak of the sheer length of the workday) can be daunting, as well as stimulating. But the greatest challenge, I believe, is to live between the Scylla and Charybdis of repetitiousness versus fragmentation. That is, we all know "Johnny one-note" colleagues who become too identified with one particular issue.

Their teaching, supervising, writing, and (probably) clinical work has that consistency that has been aptly called the hobgoblin of little minds. I remember a teacher who saw one particular form of psychopathy everywhere, so that when he began to speak at a meeting most in the audience could anticipate the gist of his remark.

Although this repetition looks like integrity it lacks soul. It isn't an alive, spontaneous, and centered response. At the other end of the spectrum are those who stand for nothing discernable. We can associate no issue with their names. They may, in fact, take contradictory positions on an issue at different occasions, without recognizing or dealing with the contradiction. This suggests to me that their opinions do not spring from a value system integral to their lives. Most of us begin our careers "shooting from the hip," clinically, as well as theoretically. Without systematic attention we allow ourselves to have our Kohutian sessions, our Sullivanian hours, and so on. I find that most clinicians can tolerate this up to a point but gradually develop a strong need to feel a clearer sense of what they are doing. I think most of us graduated from degree programs (e.g., doctorate in psychology) without having developed a personal style of treatment or a commitment to a particular theoretical framework. Professional identity development is as gradual a process as personal identity development, often with similar upheavals (Buechler, 1988). The outcome of it should be a kind of integrity, a more formulated sense of what one stands for. This signature should be apparent in all we do, not as a compulsive slogan, but as a theme and variations.

Nothing human is alien to me. That is, it *is* an important goal of any treatment to recognize and accept inner diversity. To see my own selfishness, childishness, sadism is humbling. It may help me identify more fully with others. I will be able to feel implicated in more of the range of human experience. But I don't believe this appreciation for inner diversity inspires us. That takes the kind of resonance my physically disabled analyst had. She brought everything she knew about life into the work. Whether she had gotten an idea from Emily Dickenson, Freud, or her own personal experience made no difference. It was the usefulness of the idea that mattered. I believe there is a patterned beauty and simplicity when the content and form of a message match. This matching communicates that both spring from strong personal conviction. Whatever my analyst advocated, she also lived by. This integrity gave her impact the power to inspire.

To return to the candidate who was disturbed that my point of view didn't match her other supervisor's, I believe that my first responsibility as a supervisor is to maintain my own integrity. However lonely that may leave me, I still must counter the urge in myself to pander. It would be easy for me to "fudge" and smooth over the differences between my point of view and the other supervisor's. I could emphasize the (real) commonalities. I could simply fail to underline our (equally real) differences. But then I would miss this chance to work on the issue of integrity with my supervisee. Supervision is an odd, hybrid relationship, as has been noted many times (Caligor, Bromberg, and Meltzer, 1984). It bears resemblances to treatment (especially in the work on countertransference) and to teaching (especially in some of the work on the frame). There are many potential integrity problems for each participant. As a supervisor do I care most about my "reputation," and want to be chosen often? This consideration could tempt me to pander or just fail to clearly highlight the less popular aspects of my point of view.

Here is a sample of the losses that I believe would result:

1. My troubled supervisee would miss a chance to learn how theoretical differences can translate into different clinical choices.

2. Both of us would miss an important, and perhaps mutually educative, experience. We would not get to ask each other why our interchange felt so lonely. We wouldn't get to speculate about integrity themes in treatment that might be repeating in the supervision. We wouldn't see how the wish to be liked was affecting us both.

3. We would miss a chance to manifest the struggle to achieve integrity. Specifically, in this situation, this led to asking why integrity seemed to come at such a high interpersonal price, in both the treatment and the supervision. I asked why I felt so lonely and why the candidate felt so pressured to "side" with either supervisor. How did there come to be two "sides"? Why did each of us feel that maintaining our integrity meant voicing something simply unacceptable to the other person?

4. Integrity, in the sense of wholeness, means to me that I must try to be true to all my senses. I must not deny those that challenge inner and outer harmony. I believe that this is in the spirit of Erich Fromm, who said (1968), "Because I have eyes, I have the need to see; because I have ears, I have the need to hear; because I have a mind, I have the need to think; and because I have a heart, I have the need to feel" (p. 72).

If the supervisee tells me all her conflicting feelings and I voice mine, we may meet. Something unpredictable may happen. It may lead to greater clarity about the participants in both the treatment and supervisory processes. By striving for wholeness *and* bringing up what does not jibe, we live out the challenge integrity poses for us all. Accepting the resulting jaggedness says, "It might be easier for us both if I thought X, but I think Y." By not censoring provocative news, by voicing "unfitting" parts that don't easily blend (internally or externally), we manifest the struggle for integrity. Integrity to me is a wholeness that continuously triumphs over fragmentation. Quintessentially, it is not the easy companionship of, for example, a candidate and supervisor who usually see eye to eye. In its purest form, it is the hard-won integration of hearts, minds, and souls that register differently. When a treatment or a supervision is going well, each participant constantly forges, loses, and regains this integrity. Listening to fine chamber music we hear the violin's voice and also the viola's. Each is steadfastly distinct and true enough to itself that the effort to integrate them can produce beautiful music.

9   *Emotional Uses of Theory*

Our theories do more than engage us intellectually. They fortify us emotionally, enabling us to continue working analytically. I believe we do our best work when we feel adequate hope, courage, purpose, curiosity, integrity, ability to bear loss, and capacity to modulate our other affective responses. But our balance is often upset by the inherent difficulties of doing treatment. We suffer all kinds of losses, directly and vicariously. The potential to be overwhelmed by the work's emotional intensity and complexity is enormous. We are easily flooded by affect and deluged with information. We are the repositories of countless memories, unspeakable horrors, painful secrets. Our own outrage, terror, sadness, and discouragement are often triggered. How do our theories help us stay the course?

Particularly since the rise of postmodernism, theory itself has been sharply questioned. Categorizations of all kinds have been under fire. Diagnosing patients is seen as reductionistic pigeonholing. Technique is viewed as mechanistic, stultifying. Theory creates tunnel vision, obscures real ambiguities, oversimplifies (for an extremely interesting discussion of this, see Levenson, 1991). Moreover, theory is subjective, embraced for personal reasons (Friedman, 1988). Theory is the

---

The original idea for a chapter of this kind was contributed by Paul Stepansky, Ph.D.

authority we call on to validate our personal biases, thus elevating them to the status of objective truths.

These criticisms of theory have been consciousness-raising and necessary. To me, however, they are like a medication's warning label: they are important cautions to heed, but they don't generally mean we shouldn't take the medicine at all.

Our theories enable us to bear doing treatment (for a candid example, see McCleary, 1992). As I elaborate in this chapter, regardless of its content, theory fulfills certain emotional needs of the clinician, but each theory also fortifies us in specific ways. Each has a particular effect on our emotional balance, as we conduct treatment. Each theorist, in other words, as a companion, provides a unique mix of permissions, emotional reinforcements, and intellectual rewards. Some especially strengthen our determined zeal, courage, or hope. Others free us from excess anger, shame, or guilt, enabling us to use ourselves without impediment. Some help us coalesce our sense of purpose, or integrity. In other words, while all theory affects us similarly in some senses, each also uniquely affects the clinician's balance of emotions. As Friedman (1988) inquires, "What does it *do* to a therapist to hold an idea like this?" (p. 87).

Of course any distinction between theories is not absolute. For example, although Fromm may especially promote our "prophetic" zeal, that is not all he does, and other theorists may contribute to our zeal, too. Nevertheless, I believe we can identify how each theorist most especially affects our use of our countertransference passions. This chapter proceeds from the general to the specific. I first consider how all theory helps us to do treatment, and then I suggest what particular theorists especially provide. While I emphasize its coalescing strengths, I also mention some of the dangers of reliance on theory as a treatment ally. Interpersonalists, in particular, have a long history of wariness about theory, and the dangers of a stereotyped, formulaic approach (Hirsch, 2002, has provided a succinct summary of some interpersonalists' attitudes toward theory).

A Sense of Direction

A supervisee has become dispirited, demoralized by managed care, the bureaucratization of treatment, and its effect on her practice. She has lost her sense of purpose and conviction. She feels as though she is selling something few want to buy, and even she questions its worth.

Engaging her theoretically may help awaken her to her work. Making the connection between a theory and the clinical moment it illuminates can help the clinician feel authentically involved. It provides a sense of integrity and wholeness in that mind, heart, and spirit are all engaged. It suggests a direction and therefore creates a sense of purpose. The feasibility of the goal may evoke courage and hope. Theory tells us where we are going, why, and, sometimes, how to get there. It also adds curiosity to our emotional balance and interest to our work in that everything that happens can be understood from a new angle. It adds depth and personal resonance. Clinicians often test theories on themselves at first. Reading Guntrip (1969) I might first ask, does he explain me, to me? Does it feel right? And does it help me understand my patients better? Later, as I conduct a session and think of Guntrip, a host of personal associations comes to mind. Guntrip has bridged the gap between the patient and my own experience as a human being. This adds dimensions to what I experience clinically, lending it depth and personal meaning. By enlivening the material, it prevents boredom and burnout. Another way to see this is that I can feel I am getting several things for myself, from the session. I am understanding an aspect of myself better, as well as the patient, and enriching myself intellectually as I connect the clinical moment with a theoretical concept. Connecting theory and practice can give us an expansive, fulfilled feeling. Friedman (1988) concluded, after his extensive review of the uses of theory, that psychotherapy will "thrive where theory and practice do their intricate dance" (p. 563).

Thus theory raises curiosity and affects what we notice and how we inquire, thereby shaping the material for both participants. I privilege observations of what affects the patient's anxiety level, if I think avoiding anxiety is crucial to human beings. Perhaps more important, theory shapes what is so commonplace to me that I may not notice it at all. Although this creates blind spots, it also narrows our focus enough for us to be able to work. We would be overwhelmed all the time if we tried to attend to everything occurring in a clinical hour. Theory directs us by emphasizing some aspects over others. It tells us what is most relevant, legitimizing a set of priorities.

Of course what theories we hold and how we hold them depends on who we are as people. Perhaps it is more important to be able to hold theory lightly than it is to choose theories carefully. This could facilitate correcting distortions, omissions, biases. Adherence to a "school" is like belonging to a particular culture. It shapes vision and highlights aspects of experience, leaving others in the shadows. Regardless of the school, some are rabid adherents, others are loosely identified with a school, and still others never find conviction in a belief system, out of a preference for eclecticism or a failure to attach to a theory.

Thus by acting as a filter, theory makes clinical experience possible, heightening curiosity about some aspects at the expense of others. Curiosity molds focus, and focus sorts figure from ground. By saving us from being overwhelmed by our clinical experience, theory allows us to be excited by it. Aside from saving us from chaos, theory gives us a set of categories for sorting clinical experiences. Any science has to start by naming. If I think I am in the presence of an instance of Guntrip's (1969) "need–fear dilemma," for example, then I can

1. Ignore non–need–fear aspects of this moment, thereby making it manageable.
2. Notice need–fear in myself and the patient, helping me connect.
3. Feel curiosity, wondering what evoked this response.
4. Orient toward eventual resolution of the dilemma.
5. Connect this moment with others I have known (by myself, with this patient, with other people, in the patient's history, in the patient's dreams, etc.).
6. Become exhilarated that I am learning something. Concept and moment make each other real. Mind becomes passionate, and feeling takes thoughtful shape.

Selective interest enables me to feel curiosity and communicate it to the patient. Similarly the patient can become a source of curiosity, a mine of energy that excites me. When the patient's interest spotlights aspects of our experience and my curiosity (partly shaped by theory) does the same, we both enliven each other. For us both, this may tip the balance of our emotions. Anxiety, anger, envy, shame, guilt, loneliness, and sadness recede as curiosity catches fire. Along with curiosity hope may also flourish when theory helps us make some sense of our clinical experience. In reducing chaos, theory gives each moment shape. We feel less fractured, more purposeful, and therefore more hopeful (see chapter 2).

So far I have emphasized positive uses of theory. What about its rigidifying, stultifying effects? What about how it can narrow our vision, obliterating the potential for surprise? This is what I take from Bion's (1977) oft-quoted advice to enter every session without memory or desire. Theory, by pointing us in a particular direction, pulls us *toward* memory and desire.

Perhaps like fire, theory is inherently neither positive nor negative. Its effect depends on how it is used. Do we use it to open our eyes wider, eventually questioning the very assumptions that are allowing us to function? Or is it a Procrustean bed as, I feel, Freud's oedipal theory became? The strength of theory is identical to its weakness. It concentrates attention on a part of the "woods." We don't get lost as easily, so we eventually emerge from the woods, but we may also miss out on the joys of wandering.

Just Add Water

Therapists and patients often have relationships "undreamed of in our philosophies" (many have commented on this, including Sandler, 1983, and Mitchell, 1988). It is well known, by now, that the real human interchange in treatment can look a lot different from our textbook image of it. Patients request, and often receive, direct "education" for living. What may be less obvious is the parallel occurrence in supervision. Quite similarly, supervisees are regularly given direct advice. Here, too, such "gratifications" may be proscribed by the book, but fledgling clinicians can be extremely creative in soliciting concrete direction, just as patients can be adept at extracting advice in treatment.

There are few processes more likely than supervision to bring out obsessive trends in all concerned. The clinician often desperately seeks the right word to say to the patient who, stymied by her life, is even more desperate for concrete help. How can the inexperienced clinician resist becoming obsessive and searching for rules about what to say and do? Treatment and supervision inevitably evoke everyone's anxiety, heightening obsessive (intellectualized and perfectionistic) tendencies.

But we don't want to be purveyors of cookbooks, whether as clinicians or supervisors. There is no recipe for doing treatment or for doing life. Nevertheless, particularly early in one's clinical career, doing treatment feels like such a grave responsibility, clinical hours can be so trying, the yearning for clarity can be so insistent that it seems cruel, to the supervisor, to refuse to answer the question, "What would *you* do?"

Theories differ in how specific and concrete their guidelines are. With some we have to work hard to derive their recommendations. With others clinical behavior is all but dictated, our words chosen for us. It seems to me that both of these extremes can be demoralizing.

From my point of view, the best theories give us unforgettable, evocative phrases. These words don't come with a set of directions as to just when and how to apply them. Thinking of these words remains an alive response to a particular clinical moment, not a deadened formulaic exercise.

Examples would be Guntrip's "need–fear dilemma," Winnicott's "capacity to be alone," Klein's "depressive position," Sullivan's "participant observation," and Kohut's "empathic failure." Each of these offers companionship at certain potentially lonely moments for the clinician. They don't tell her what to say, or when to say it, but they do suggest something she might be thinking about.

Sullivanian Participant Observation

From my own, largely Sullivanian training, I took something more coherent than a set of phrases. Based on Sullivan's *The Psychiatric Interview* (1954) and other writings (1940, 1953, 1956), I learned what Levenson (1982) might call an algorithm of treatment. It included frame setting, extensive history taking early in the work, detailed inquiry to clarify interpersonal patterns, evocative summarizing to elicit curiosity, and, finally, termination.

This regimen addresses several key countertransferential emotions, especially the clinician's obsessive anxiety, as discussed earlier. Sullivanian history taking and participant-observation give the clinician something clear to do while the transference develops. Sullivan has always been known for his focus on the patient's anxiety, but I am emphasizing how his approach calms the clinician's anxiety, most especially the obsessive variety. It tames the overwhelming sea of possibilities. History taking creates a "correct" order. Chronology structures the early treatment discourse. Learning about the patient's adolescence structurally follows exploring her childhood.

The clinician's obsessive anxiety about getting treatment "right" is further allayed by Sullivan's portrayal of the role of the "expert" and by his suggestion to track fluctuations in the patient's anxiety. Treatment takes on the flavor of research, with each intervention a hypothesis, followed by observation of its impact on the patient's level of anxiety. The clinician's task can be defined, described, and accomplished. Taking histories becomes familiar and lends the work a coherent structure. The role of the expert confers authority. Tracking anxiety focuses our minds and suggests we are having an impact. History taking, tracking anxiety, defining interpersonal patterns, inquiring about their repetition, and observing one's own participation are all possible. Here are tasks to which the clinician can apply herself, that require alertness, organization, and effort. Some will perform them with greater ease and intuitive facility, and greater experience enhances their familiarity, but even the novice can feel at least minimally competent in these tasks.

Other needs of the clinician are satisfied by the Sullivanian approach. It has an egalitarian, democratic, respectful feel, treating people as "more human than otherwise," regardless of their level of pathology. The clinician can experience herself as a good, democratic, tolerant person. This approach also engenders *hope*. American mid–20th-century optimism about self-improvement is built into the Sullivanian framework. This system suggests that so long as one profits from new experience, problems can be solved. I believe that the inability to profit from new experience is Sullivan's fundamental conception of pathology. This implies a kind of faith in human resourcefulness. Freed from "parataxic distortions" human beings can tackle their lives. This hopefulness can help the clinician believe that patterns can be elucidated, problems can be solved, patients can be helped, and, for the clinician herself, clinical mastery can be achieved.

This approach also fosters a sense of integrity in the clinician. We don't feel fraudulent with the role of expert, and with tasks that can be accomplished. Using a Sullivanian paradigm, we can integrate lessons from our personal life experiences into our work. Our own lives provide ample illustrations of what can heighten anxiety, as well as what might mitigate it. Knowing we are all "more simply human" encourages us to use our own experience to try to understand the patient, whether she is neurotically anxious or psychotically confused. The clinician in us is seamlessly fused with the patient, adolescent, wife, and so on, making an integrated whole.

There are also dangers in adhering to the Sullivanian paradigm. Its "can-do" philosophy doesn't fit every situation. I think it may contribute to the clinician's exasperation with some patients. Farber (1966), for example, doesn't sound too keen on hysterics:

> I would maintain that far from being a prelude or a preparation, hysteria is passion's deadly adversary; hysteria loathes passion as a potential usurper of its usurped domain. With similar shrewdness it abhors wit, discrimination, imagination, humor, and judgment—all those aspects of intelligence whose injury and impairments are its goal and result. It is true that we must live with hysteria, but we need not, I think, honor it. In fact, if we give it its rightful identification as the sworn enemy of our capacity to be fully human, we may give ourselves a crucial advantage in the struggle we must constantly engage in to transcend it [p. 117].

Nor did Sullivan have an overflow of respect for these patients: "What you see in the hysteric is thus not a high-grade conflict between ideal structures and unregenerated impulses, but just a happy idea of how to get away with something" (1956, p. 204); "hysterics may be said to be the greatest liars to no purpose in the whole range of human personalities" (p. 209).

The Sullivanian worldview best suits the hardworking clinician with an inhibited but hardworking patient. Both are showing American pluck, making the most they can of themselves, plugging along like "little engines that could." Unlike the hysteric who is seen with contempt, the frightened, lonely, bright but socially limited schizoid obsessional, for example, seems to yearn to join the human fold, and will do so, if helped to overcome his obstacles.

But what of those who, for one reason or another, resist progress? I don't think Sullivan gives us a way of working with them. Even an obsessional who balks at change can elicit his barely contained wrath. As noted in an earlier chapter, to one patient frightened of his own impulse to fling himself down the hospital stairs, a clearly exasperated Sullivan declared (1956), "I am transferring you to the second floor now, and issuing orders that you will not be served a tray. And so, I don't know; maybe you will die by flinging yourself over the stairs;

I doubt it. Maybe you will starve to death; I doubt that too. But we'll have to see" (p. 259).

Sullivan doesn't help us inhabit certain dark sides. His thinking could exacerbate blaming depressives for willful stasis, hysterics for deliberate dramatic distortion, and narcissists for selfish intrapersonal preoccupation. Sullivan doesn't tolerate gladly those who feel too "special" to be "more simply human than otherwise."

When I am working clinically, I find Sullivan a wonderful companion. He is especially helpful to me when I am trying to reach a profoundly lonely, cutoff patient, who missed out on the gratifications of an interpersonal life but still yearns for them.

Of course Sullivanian theory, like all theory, focuses us selectively, making us more likely to miss some things. Believing in the power of environmental input, and self-determination, and the luck of the interpersonal draw, we may not easily recognize the inborn equipment that delimits achievement. By giving us the concepts of "selective attention" and "selective inattention," Sullivan helped us name what can happen when his (or any other) theory is applied in practice.

In clearly defining our task as helping people become able to learn from new experience (1953, 1954) Sullivan decreased the clinician's confusion and anxiety. This makes change, and therefore hope, seem possible. He also helps the clinician heighten his own curiosity, which further changes the balance of his emotions. The emphasis on questions, inquiry, expanding, and elaborating the data has been adopted by post-Sullivanian interpersonalists (Hirsch, 2002). Levensonian technique, for example, encourages the clinician to wonder, "What happened to the cat?" That is, how can we use our own curiosity to highlight the details that have been left out of the patient's account of his life? Once this is established, how can we make coherent sense out of why these details were selectively inattended? The clinician's curiosity is encouraged and prized in this process.

Thus our anxiety is reduced by the clarity and expert status of our role. Helping people become able to learn from their experience gives us a sense of purpose. The universality of anxiety encourages us to identify with our patients' travails. Taking a history gives us a structured, doable task and reveals the patient as someone who also had a first day of school. We can use our own personal experience with life, which allows us the integrity of bringing our whole selves to our work. Clinician and patient, using curiosity, create a coherent story, all the while noticing the difficulties they encounter. A can-do spirit, a basic optimism, and an emphasis on nurture over nature contribute to a heightened self-esteem and sense of possibility, for both participants. In this relatively sunny world, the clinician can shed self-doubt, feelings of hollow fraudulence, guilt, and shame. Restoring patients to our "more simply human" world gives us purpose, courage, integrity, and, perhaps most of all, hope.

Frieda Fromm-Reichmann, deeply influenced by Sullivan, used his understanding of anxiety to deal with her own responses to patients. In her biography of Fromm-Reichmann, Hornstein (2000) reports:

> Like Ferenczi and Sullivan, Frieda said that a therapist couldn't be effective with psychotic patients if he were frightened of them. She understood why staff would feel this way, but urged them "to stay away from patients of whom they are afraid" to avoid intensifying their patients' anguish. If possible, the therapist should examine the "unconscious reasons for his anxiety" and try to overcome it. "The psychiatrist or the nurse [who] wants to continue work with a patient despite fear should speak about it with the patient. Once the therapist is aware and not ashamed of his fear, and is free to make it a topic of discussion with the patient, it [need] not interfere with his usefulness" [pp. 168–169].

Thus Fromm-Reichmann was advocating that the clinician should monitor shifts in his own anxiety level, just as Sullivan (1954) recommended we monitor the patient's anxiety. In this advice I see her as (perhaps not consciously) connecting two Sullivanian principles: the emphasis on anxiety and the emphasis on interpersonal impact. Interestingly she also uses her understanding of the emotions as forming a system, in her advice on how the clinician can manage his feelings. If we can conquer shame about fear, Fromm-Reichmann suggests, the fear itself will not be debilitating.

Later (p. 169), Fromm-Reichmann gives this example from her own clinical experience:

> A patient hit me and asked me the next day whether or not I resented his having done so. My answer was that I did not mind his hitting me as such because I realized that he was too inarticulate to express, other than by action, the well-founded resentment he felt against me at the time. "However," I went on, "I do

resent being hurt as everyone does; moreover, if I must watch lest I get hurt, my attention will be distracted from following with alertness the content of your communications." The patient responded by promising spontaneously not to hit me again, and he kept his promise despite several hostile phases through which he was still to progress.

Thus, Fromm-Reichmann had absorbed Sullivan's belief about the effect of anxiety on cognition and used it in her appeal to the patient.

I would say that the legacies of Sullivan and Fromm-Reichmann mesh well. Her determined, humanistic, fighting spirit complements his active, monitoring stance. When these influences combine I think they foster clinical stamina, especially for the work with extremely disturbed patients.

The Zealous Prophet

Fromm has been lauded and criticized for his passion as a prophetic missionary. Maccoby (1996), who was in treatment with him, bluntly described how the prophet in Fromm interfered with the functioning of the analyst. We can see the strengths as well as the drawbacks of passionate zeal when we examine the impact Fromm had as an analyst, supervisor, and theoretician.

For Fromm (1973) what is done to promote fully living life is good. Some of his book titles express his most cherished values: *Man for Himself* (1947), *The Sane Society* (1955), *The Art of Loving* (1956), *The Heart of Man: Its Genius for Good and Evil* (1964b), *To Have or to Be* (1976), *For the Love of Life* (a compilation of radio talks Fromm gave in his last years, transcribed in 1986). Fromm encourages us to fight for freedom and self-actualization, in ourselves and in our patients. Fully living is a goal worth striving for. We should embrace, and not escape our freedom as human beings. We are here to promote life passionately and tend our own life force. He validates the true-believing, courageous, full-hearted preacher in us.

I think Fromm can whip up our anger at wasted potential. He gives us a strong sense of purpose, hope, courage, and integrity. We feel we are fighting the good fight, on the side of the angels. On the positive side this can contribute to our stamina, holding us steady during periods of treatment stasis or regression. It may help us tolerate the patient's confusion, doubt, skepticism, even contempt. We have conviction in our mission. We can feel centered and whole.

The dangers of this attitude were, I feel, amply demonstrated by Fromm himself. His passionate stance can obliterate nuance and ambiguity, and destroy what is valuable in neutrality. We can become so convinced we know what is good for people that we ride roughshod over them, preaching a way of life that has more to do with our own prejudices than the patient's welfare. We can think we know more than it is possible for one human being to decide about how another should live. Fanaticism easily breeds in this atmosphere. Take, for example, one of the few published accounts by Fromm (1964a) of his own clinical work, in which he "cured" a woman of homosexual desires.

Fromm encourages the clinician's anger, contempt, and impatience with what he calls (1973) "necrophilic" forces. This profoundly affects the clinician's emotional and interpretive balance. Interpretively this privileges material that helps us fight on the side of the "biophilic" or life-enhancing pulls. Nuance and ambivalence have no place in such a war. Fighting for life itself eclipses other tendencies. Doubts, worries, and uncertainties don't seem worth attention. In both participants preserving pride, dwelling on sources of guilt, even anxieties fade in significance. All else pales when life itself is at stake. This is adaptive, in that the treatment participants become allies, mobilized in the fight against necrophilia. Troops are rallied, spirits soar. But in wartime civil rights can be eroded. In the passionate fight for the patient's life we may lose sight of her unique vision, and the limitations of our own.

Showing All Your Cards

Building on the work of Sullivan, Thompson, Fromm-Reichmann, and others, interpersonalists have developed an orientation with its own guiding ideals (Lionells et al., 1995):

> Interpersonal psychoanalysis is, at once, a repudiation of orthodox biologism and clinical dogma and a rejection of reified notions of psychic structure. It is essentially pragmatic, flexible, and down-to-earth because it deals with what actually transpires between people and how they live (and structure) that experience. Interpersonal writings are generally couched in

everyday, nonjargonistic language. Interpersonal theory addresses more or less the same body of phenomena addressed by other schools of psychoanalytic thought, but it does so without the reification of metaphors that is so common to psychoanalysis [p. 4].

This approach has fostered experimental uses of the countertransference. There are many examples of the courage this way of working requires, and stimulates. Of course leading this list is Ferenczi, whose self-inquiry was relentless (Dupont, 1988, p. 194): "I do not know of any analyst whose analysis I could declare, theoretically, as concluded (least of all of my own). Thus we have, in every single analysis, quite enough to learn about ourselves." Other examples include Wolstein's (1975, 1987) use of the concept of "cocreation," Ehrenberg's (1992) exploration of the "intimate edge," and Levenson's inquiry into "what is going on" interpersonally (for a summary of this literature, see Hirsch, 1995).

The inward focus has its emotional consequences. Some facilitate the work, and others impede it. For example, an emphasis on the countertransference can augment a self-flagellating tendency if it already exits. Hornstein (2000) sees this as a problem for Fromm-Reichmann:

However, Ferenczi's admission that his own negative countertransference feelings could be a factor in the patient's resistance also encouraged Frieda's lifelong tendency to blame herself when things went wrong in her relationships. Up to a point, this was helpful because it protected patients from having to bear the burden of her inadequacies. But taken too far, this attitude of holding the doctor responsible for every treatment failure threatened to fill psychiatrists with so much guilt they became useless to their patients. Frieda was well aware of this danger; she constantly struggled to follow Ferenczi's lead and use countertransference feelings as a subtle source of information rather than a means of self-flagellation [p. 45].

On the other hand, I think it may also help us bear concentrating on the welfare of others, for so many hours a day.

Two forms the interpersonal emphasis on countertransference has taken are disclosure of autobiographical details and disclosure of emotional responses to the patient. Both require the analyst to focus inwardly, at least for the length of time it takes to formulate the disclosure. Each requires the analyst to be willing to be known. The psychological availability they require is different, however, and each of the two types of disclosure seems likely to recruit its own set of emotions. This means they will have somewhat different impacts on the analyst's emotional balance. Telling a patient about my life outside the analysis would affect me differently from telling a patient she just elicited my anxiety.

There is a rapidly accumulating literature on all kinds of countertransference disclosure (e.g., Blechner, 1992; Hoffman, 1983, 1998; Maroda, 1999; Renik, 1995). What to disclose, how, and when have all but replaced the question of whether to disclose at all. Disclosing affects the analyst's feelings in many ways, not the least of which is its impact on the clinician's loneliness, as I discuss shortly. I believe, however, that the impact on our shame, guilt, and anxiety is no less significant, although it may be less obvious. In addition, although disclosure would be likely to impact the sense of courage and integrity, it is less clear how it would affect hope and the sense of purpose. Finally, it seems plausible that disclosure would play a role in how the loss of the relationship affects both participants at termination. I briefly address each of these sequelae in the rest of this chapter.

For one thing, some personal disclosures can profoundly affect our loneliness. If it is our job to disclose our responses to the patient, we are less likely to be lonely, in the usual sense of the term. Loneliness has been defined (Fromm-Reichmann, 1959) as the feeling of permanent aloneness. Thus, whether I feel lonely when alone depends on how permanent I believe my condition to be. The cognitive and the emotional are profoundly intertwined in this conception.

The clinician is inherently less lonely if she believes she will not always be alone with her experience of the treatment (Buechler, 1998). The resulting benefits for the clinician have received less attention than the advantages for the patient. In "Hate in the Countertransference," for example, Winnicott (1949) advises us that a treatment isn't finished for the patient until he understands what the clinician had to bear for the sake of their work.

Looking at a different kind of disclosure, the clinician who discloses personal autobiographical information may feel heightened shame in that there is greater potential for the feeling of self-exposure.

Greater openness could trigger a fear of shame, or actual shame, in being revealed to the patient, warts and all.

Anxiety in the clinician also may be heightened to the extent that any personal information or an emotional reaction to the patient is shared before it is understood, or " processed." That is, it can create anxiety to begin a disclosure without knowing where it may lead. Although this may also stimulate curiosity and surprise (in both participants), it may increase the anxiety that can sometimes accompany us into the unknown (Izard, 1977).

For example, in a moving article on her experience of having breast cancer, Kahn (2003) wrestles with the issue of self-disclosure. Whose need was she serving when she judged it better "for the patient" to disclose her illness? Kahn gives evidence on all sides, illustrating disclosures that seemed to benefit one or both participants and some that seemed to do harm. Among disclosure's effects was an *increase,* at times, in Kahn's anxiety level. She cites Aron (1996), who confirms that self-disclosure can lead to increased anxiety in the analyst. He cites Wachtel (1993) and Hoffman (1994), who proposed that *limiting* self-disclosure sometimes increases the analyst's ability to tolerate the patient. In a similar vein, it is widely known that Freud, almost a century earlier, adopted the use of the couch as standard analytic technique to limit his exposure to patients—to remove himself from the anxiety provoked by his patient's scrutiny.

Among many others, Karen Maroda (1991, 1999, 2002) has argued persuasively in favor of disclosure of our emotional reactions to patients. She is explicit about her belief that it benefits both participants. Yet she has also been eloquent about some of its quagmires, and, most especially, because it emphasizes the ultimate subjectivity of all human experience, its inherent anxiety for the practitioner:

> Finally, all the things we were actually experiencing with patients were being said out loud. We were off the hook for not being perfect. And we were freed from trying to practice in ways that did not work very well. We could stop being authoritarian, rude, and withholding. We could be human beings and analysts at the same time. This trend toward humanizing the analytic process and acknowledging the inherent mutuality seemed unstoppable.
>
> But lately the tide seems to be turning. People who were comfortable with acknowledging the patient as interpreter of

the analyst's experience are not so comfortable with the notion of everything that happens in the room as mutually cocreated and implicitly unknowable. As the two-person position relies heavily on a philosophical perspective rather than a pragmatic one, some clinicians find their relief turning into confusion, anxiety, and frustration. It seems that once we admitted to our countertransference and the mutuality of the therapeutic relationship, we did not have a clear idea of how it should be handled in the consulting room [2002, pp. 101–102].

Just a bit later Maroda (2002) states the situation emphatically:

We are unnerved by the thought that nothing is absolutely knowable. We do not like questioning everything we think and feel about the patient. And we certainly do not like going from the position that we know everything to the position that we cannot absolutely know *anything*. Reluctant to prescribe any new techniques, we failed to translate adequately our theoretical revisions into new clinical practice rooted in theory. Using one's intuition may work for experienced, master clinicians, but how can we teach our approach to young clinicians looking for guidelines and hands-on information? [p. 102].

I think in any self-revealing venture there can also be a spirit of repentance, in the sense of making up for the sins of our analytic fathers. Some of our classical forbears imposed their ungratifying method unyieldingly. They insisted on their right to remain silent, certainly, at least, about themselves. Those were the bad old days. We aren't like them. We aren't aloof and superior any more.

Aside from being a less guilty, lonely position, from our being less *fearful* of shame but perhaps more vulnerable to shame and anxiety, I wonder if the disclosing stance truncates aggressive feelings in both participants, especially if what is disclosed is information about the analyst's life. The disclosing clinician is too human to hate. How can anyone even be angry at such a modest egalitarian? Disclosure atones for both our collective and personal hubris. It is hard to be angry at the prodigal analyst, eagerly rejoining the human fold. Disclosing personal information makes the statement that we do not hold ourselves above the fray. Of course it is possible that we are actually regaining our feelings of moral superiority by "sacrificing" authoritarian advantages. But it is also possible that genuine integrity or wholeness results from disclosures that decrease the gap between our professional and private selves.

Personally revealing disclosure allows the clinician to "go first" in refusing to be intimidated by fear of shame. This may be especially effective with narcissistic patients. It tells the patient that he is not the only one with uncertainty, defensive avoidance, human limitations. In a way, it provides benefits similar to those offered by group therapy—the opportunity for the patient to compare himself to someone else, see the human condition for what it is, feel less alone, ashamed, and aberrant. A kind of esprit de corps can develop, a feeling of all being "in it" together, fighting common human difficulties.

These potentially inspiring moments can reveal the clinician's effortful dedication to the work. Her sense of its purpose and value is palpable in the decision to reveal something personal that may not be easy to say. It implicitly states that, to the clinician, their work is worth this effort. Thus it models these values, making the patient's self-disclosures easier and more natural. In this atmosphere mutual disclosures can begin to feel inevitable. It probably always feels more natural to be naked in the company of other naked people.

At the same time as the disclosing analyst is providing a model of effort, honesty, courage, and integrity, he is also relieving himself of some of the strain of separating what is appropriate to say from what is inappropriate. I feel this is analogous to Winnicottian transitional space, where culture provides relief from the work of separating external from internal. Disclosure transforms treatment into a space where the internal can be made external, shared, played with together. Just as watching a play or looking at a painting I don't have to worry too much about what is coming from the painting versus what is coming from me, similarly, in moments of disclosure thoughts are valued for being interesting and evoking curiosity more than for their "appropriateness." In this space, the relevance of thoughts to the treatment cannot easily be discerned before they are tossed around. A looser, more playful creativity is manifested and encouraged by the disclosing clinician. This stance probably heightens curiosity and the role of surprise, and lowers guilt in both participants as they create an atmosphere in which thoughts can be freely considered, revised, kept, or thrown away. Here the origin of the thought doesn't matter. Whether it comes from the clinician's or the patient's personal or professional experience or their mutual experience, what counts is whether the thought is interesting,

novel, or potentially useful. Disclosure is a way for the clinician to es-
cort the patient into this space. Freeing himself from being con-
strained by his role, the disclosing clinician is valuing the thought for
itself. He is not inhibited by potential shame or anxiety or guilt about
breaking rules. By disclosing we say the treatment is worth taking
these chances. We are, thus, behaviorally commenting on what matters most, on risk itself, and on our feelings about this particular treatment's safety level *for us.*

So where does the self-disclosing clinician affectively stand? What
can we promise supervisees and students who adopt this approach? I
would say that they will probably encounter less of the patient's aggression, and more of their own shame and anxiety than their less self-disclosing colleagues. They may feel less guilty about their hubris, less
lonely, and less intimidated by the fear of shame. They will have taken
a chance, betting on modeling a courageous relationship to risk, one
that optimizes the integrity of bringing together personal and professional, into an integrated whole. Sparks will fly, curiosity, the edge of
danger, will be felt. And the treatment relationship may be harder to
let go of, at termination, for both participants. But will the clinician
ever feel confident, secure, competent? Will she ever feel she knows
what she is doing? I think we might all join Maroda (2002), who cautions, "If the two-person approach is to survive and continue to influence new generations of therapists, we must empower clinicians with
techniques that are solidly grounded in theory and research. We must
give them techniques they can master and that work" (p. 118).

Just as Bettelheim reminded us, years ago, that love is not (always)
enough, the prescription to disclose affectively leaves the clinician at
the mercy of her anxiety, and therefore license to disclose is also not
enough. We have convinced neophytes and most others that all human
experience, including the clinician's, is subjective. Disclosing is the response to this knowledge that many now take. Although exciting, this
situation opens us up to the dreads of the inherently unknowable, the
shame of self-exposure, the anxiety of incompetence. We can envision
what we left behind much more clearly than what we want to become.
Proud of our courage, stimulated by our curiosity, we may nevertheless be unable to bear the anxious position we have ourselves created.

Sullivan's "expert" clinician knew where he was going. He tracked
anxiety, observing its fluctuation with each of his interventions. He
looked for familiar patterns in the history and in the current symp-
tomatology. He may have been limited in who he could work with

(self-preoccupied hysterics need not apply). But for the clinician competence was possible, even without a great deal of experience.

Fromm's freedom fighter could also be sure he was doing something worthwhile, struggling to enhance biophilia and root out necrophilia. His approach gives the clinician a real sense of purpose and spirit, unfettered by self-doubt. Anger at wasted life fuels his passionate mission.

Emotional balance has become more complex. Ideally, we would like to have a Sullivanian sense of competence, a Frommian passion, and a modern awareness of subjectivity, including our own. Is this possible? Probably not. But I believe it is possible for the analyst to *strive* toward balance. Like any other human being, the analyst cannot consciously control her emotions, taking anxiety down a notch and whipping up curiosity. But I believe we can manifest our struggle toward workable emotional intensities, face the inevitable moments of imbalance, and palpably fight our way back.

References

Abend, S. (1989), Countertransference and psychoanalytic technique. *Psychoanal. Quart.*, 58:374–395.

Altman, N. (2002), Where is the action in the "talking cure"? *Contemp. Psychoanal.*, 38:499–515.

Alvarez, A. (1992), *Live Company*. London and New York: Tavistock/ Routledge.

Arieti, S. (1978), The basic questions and the psychological approach. In: *Severe and Mild Depression,* ed. S. Arieti & J. Bemporad. New York: Basic Books.

Aristotle (fourth century B.C.), *The Nicomachean Ethics,* trans. H. Rackham. Ware, Hertfordshire: Wordsworth Editions.

Aron, L. (1996), *A Meeting of Minds: Mutuality in Psychoanalysis.* Hillsdale, NJ: The Analytic Press.

Barford, D. (2002), *The Ship of Thought.* London: Karnac Books.

Barnett, J. (1980), Interpersonal processes, cognition and the analysis of character. *Contemp. Psychoanal.*, 16:397–416.

Bayley, J. (1999a), Last jokes. *The New Yorker.* August 2, pp. 38–43.

———— (1999b), *Elegy for Iris.* New York: Norton.

———— (2000), *Iris and Her Friends: A Memoir of Memory and Desire.* New York: Norton.

Biancoli, R. (2002), Psychoanalyst's values and countertransference. *Internat. Forum Psychoanal.*, 2:10–18.

Bion, W. R. (1977), *Seven Servants.* New York: Aronson.

Blechner, M. J. (1992), Working in the countertransference. *Psychoanal. Dial.*, 2:161–179.

_____ (2001), *The Dream Frontier.* Hillsdale, NJ: The Analytic Press.

Bollas, C. (1987), *The Shadow of the Object.* New York: Columbia University Press.

Bose, J. (1995), Depression. In: *Handbook of Interpersonal Psychoanalysis,* ed. M. Lionells, J. Fiscalini, C. H. Mann & D. B. Stern. Hillsdale, NJ: The Analytic Press, pp. 435–469.

Bromberg, P. M. (1998), *Standing in the Spaces: Essays on Clinical Process, Trauma, and Dissociation.* Hillsdale: NJ: The Analytic Press.

Buechler, S. (1988), Joining the psychoanalytic culture. *Contemp. Psychoanal.*, 24:462–470.

_____ (1992), Stress in the personal and professional development of a psychoanalyst. *J. Amer. Acad. Psychoanal.*, 20:183–191.

_____ (1993), Clinical applications of an interpersonal view of the emotions. *Contemp. Psychoanal.*, 29:219–236.

_____ (1995a), Emotion. In: *Handbook of Interpersonal Psychoanalysis,* ed. M. Lionells, J. Fiscalini, C. H. Mann, & D. B. Stern. Hillsdale, NJ: The Analytic Press, pp. 165–188.

_____ (1995b), Hope as inspiration in psychoanalysis. *Psychoanal. Dial.*, 5:63–74.

_____ (1996), Supervision of the treatment of borderline patients. *Contemp. Psychoanal.*, 32:86–92.

_____ (1997), The right stuff. *Contemp. Psychoanal.*, 33:295–306.

_____ (1998), The analyst's experience of loneliness. *Contemp. Psychoanal.*, 34:91–115.

_____ (1999), Searching for a passionate neutrality. *Contemp. Psychoanal.*, 35:231–227.

_____ (2000), Necessary and unnecessary losses: The analyst's mourning. *Contemp. Psychoanal.*, 36:77–90.

_____ (2002a), Instigating hope in psychoanalysis. Presented at meeting of the International Forum of Psychoanalysis, Oslo, Norway.

_____ (2002b), Joy in the analytic encounter: A response to Biancoli. *Contemp. Psychoanal.*, 38:613–622.

_____ (2002c), More simply human than otherwise. *Contemp. Psychoanal.*, 38:485–497.

_____ (2003), Analytic integrity: A review of *Affect Intolerance in Patient and Analyst. Contemp. Psychoanal.*, 39:323–326.

_____ & Izard, C. E. (1980), Anxiety in childhood and adolescence. In: *Handbook on Stress and Anxiety,* ed. I. L. Kutash & L. B. Schlesinger. San Francisco: Jossey-Bass, pp. 285–298.

Burston, D. (1991), *The Legacy of Erich Fromm.* Cambridge, MA: Harvard University Press.

Caligor, L., Bromberg, P. M. & Meltzer, J. D., eds. (1984), *Clinical Perspectives on the Supervision of Psychoanalysis and Psychotherapy.* New York: Plenum Press.

Casey, N., ed. (2001), *Unholy Ghost: Writers on Depression.* New York: Harper Collins.

Chefetz, R. A. & Bromberg, P. M. (2002), Talking with "me and not-me": A dialogue. Presented at cosponsored workshop of the William Alanson White Institute and the ISSD, New York City.

Chodoff, P. (1974), The diagnosis of hysteria. *Amer. J. Psychiat.,* 131: 1073–1078.

Coen, S. (2002), *Affect Intolerance in Patient and Analyst.* Northvale, NJ: Aronson.

Coltart, N. (1993), *How to Survive as a Psychotherapist.* London: Sheldon Press.

Cooper, Allen (1969), Problems in therapy of a patient with masked depression. *Contemp. Psychoanal.,* 5:45–57.

Cooper, Arnold (1986), Some limitations of therapeutic effectiveness: "The burnout syndrome" in psychoanalysis. *Psychoanal. Quart.,* 55:576–598.

Cooper, S. H. (2000), *Objects of Hope.* Hillsdale, NJ: The Analytic Press.

Cortina, M. & Maccoby, M., eds. (1996), *A Prophetic Analyst: Erich Fromm's Contribution to Psychoanalysis.* Northvale, NJ: Aronson.

Cushman, P. (1995), *Constructing the Self, Constructing America.* Reading, MA: Addison-Wesley.

———— & Gilford, P. (1999), From emptiness to multiplicity: The self at the year 2000. *Psychohist. Rev.,* 27:15–32.

Dickens, C. (1854), *Hard Times.* New York: Harper & Row, 1954.

Dupont, J., ed. (1988), *The Clinical Diary of Sándor Ferenczi.* Cambridge, MA: Harvard University Press.

Edelson, M. (1993), Telling and enacting stories in psychoanalysis and psychotherapy. In: *The Psychoanalytic Study of the Child,* 48:293–325. New Haven, CT: Yale University Press.

Edmundson, M. (2000), Playing the fool. *New York Times Book Rev.,* April 2, p. 35.

Ehrenberg, D. B. (1992), *The Intimate Edge: Extending the Reach of Psychoanalytic Interaction.* New York: Norton.

Eliot, T. S. (1943), *Four Quartets.* New York: Harcourt.

Epstein, L. (1979), The therapeutic use of countertransference data with borderline patients. *Contemp. Psychoanal.,* 15:248–275.

———— & Feiner, A. H. (1979), *Countertransference.* Northvale, NJ: Aronson.

Farber, L. H. (1966), *The Ways of the Will.* New York: Basic Books.

Feiner, A. H. (1986), Discussion of collusive selective inattention to the negative impact of the supervisory interaction. *Contemp. Psychoanal.,* 22:409–417

Fiscalini, J. (1995), Narcissism and self-disorder. In: *Handbook of Interpersonal Psychoanalysis,* ed. M. Lionells, J. Fiscalini, C. H. Mann & D. B. Stern. Hillsdale, NJ: The Analytic Press, pp. 333–374.

Fonagy, P. (2001), *Attachment Theory and Psychoanalysis.* New York: Other Press.

Freud, A. (1936), *The Ego and the Mechanisms of Defense.* London: Karnac Books.

Freud, S. (1910), Five lectures on psychoanalysis. *Standard Edition,* 11:9–55. London: Hogarth Press, 1957.

_____ (1912), Recommendations to physicians practising psycho-analysis. *Standard Edition,* 12:111–120. London: Hogarth Press, 1958.

_____ (1915), Observations on transference-love (Further recommendations on the technique of psycho-analysis III). *Standard Edition,* 12: 159–171. London: Hogarth Press, 1958.

_____ (1916), Introductory lectures on psycho-analysis, Part III. General theory of the neurosis (1917). Lecture 27: Transference. *Standard Edition,* 16:243–463. London: Hogarth Press, 1965.

_____ (1917/1915), Mourning and melancholia. *Standard Edition.* 14:237–258. London: Hogarth Press, 1957.

_____ (1926), Inhibitions, symptoms and anxiety. *Standard Edition,* 20:87–175. London: Hogarth Press, 1959.

Friedman, L. (1988), *The Anatomy of Psychotherapy.* Hillsdale, NJ: The Analytic Press.

Fromm, E. (1941), *Escape from Freedom.* New York: Farrar & Rinehart.

_____ (1947), *Man for Himself.* New York: Rinehart.

_____ (1955), *The Sane Society.* New York: Holt, Rinehart & Winston.

_____ (1956), *The Art of Loving.* New York: Harper & Row.

_____ (1962), *Beyond the Chains of Illusion.* New York: Trident Press.

_____ (1964a), Causes for the patient's change in analytic treatment. Reprinted in *Contemp. Psychoanal.,* 27:579–602, 1991.

_____ (1964b), *The Heart of Man: Its Genius for Good and Evil.* New York: Harper & Row.

_____ (1968), *The Revolution of Hope.* New York: Harper & Row.

_____ (1973), *The Anatomy of Human Destructiveness.* New York: Holt, Rinehart & Winston.

_____ (1976), *To Have or to Be?* New York: Harper & Row.

_____ (1986), *For the Love of Life,* with H. J. Schultz. New York: Macmillan.

_____ & Maccoby, M. (1970), *Social Character in a Mexican Village.* Englewood Cliffs, NJ: Prentice-Hall.

Fromm-Reichmann, F. (1959), Loneliness. *Contemp. Psychoanal.,* 26:305–330, 1990.

Frost, R. (1943), *The Complete Poems of Robert Frost.* New York: Holt, Rinehart & Winston.

Funk, R. (1982), *Erich Fromm: The Courage to Be Human.* New York: Continuum.

_____ (2002), Psychoanalysis and human values. *Internat. Forum Psychoanal.,* 2:18–27.

Gaines, R. (1997), Detachment and continuity: The two tasks of mourning. *Contemp. Psychoanal.,* 33:549–571.

Gensler, D., Goldman, D., Goldman, D., Gordon, R. M., Prince, R. & Rosenbach, N. (2002), Voices from New York: Sept. 11, 2001. *Contemp. Psychoanal.,* 38:77–100.

Greenberg, J. (1991), *Oedipus and Beyond: A Clinical Theory.* Cambridge, MA: Harvard University Press.

Grosskurth, P. (1986), *Melanie Klein: Her World and Her Work.* New York: Knopf.

Guntrip, H. (1969), *Schizoid Phenomenon, Object-Relations and the Self.* New York: International Universities Press.

Hirsch, I. (1995), Therapeutic uses of the countertransference. In: *Handbook of Interpersonal Psychoanalysis,* ed. M. Lionells, J. Fiscalini, C. H. Mann & D. B. Stern. Hillsdale, NJ: The Analytic Press, pp. 643–661.

_____ (2002), Beyond interpretation: Analytic interaction in the interpersonal tradition. *Contemp. Psychoanal.,* 38:573–589.

Hoffman, I. Z. (1983), The patient as interpreter of the analyst's experience. *Contemp. Psychoanal.,* 19:389–422.

_____ (1987), The value of uncertainty in psychoanalytic practice. *Contemp. Psychoanal.,* 23:205–215.

_____ (1994), Dialectical thinking and therapeutic action in the psychoanalytic process. *Psychoanal. Quart.,* 63:187–218.

_____ (1998), *Ritual and Spontaneity in the Psychoanalytic Process: A Dialectical-Constructivist View.* Hillsdale, NJ: The Analytic Press.

Hornstein, G. A. (2000), *To Redeem One Person is to Redeem the World: The Life of Frieda Fromm-Reichmann.* New York: Free Press.

Issacharoff, A. (1997), A conversation with Dr. Alberta Szalita. *Contemp. Psychoanal.,* 33:615–632.

Izard, C. E. (1971), *The Face of Emotion.* New York: Meredith.

_____ (1972), *Patterns of Emotion.* New York: Academic Press.

_____ (1977), *Human Emotions.* New York: Plenum Press.

Jacobs, T. (1986), On countertransference enactments. *J. Amer. Psychoanal. Assn.,* 34:289–307.

Kahn, N. E. (2003), Self-disclosure of serious illness: The impact of boundary disruptions for patient and analyst. *Contemp. Psychoanal.,* 39:51–75.

Kantrowitz, J. L. (1996), *The Patient's Impact on the Analyst.* Hillsdale, NJ: The Analytic Press.

Kernberg, O. F. (1975), *Borderline Conditions and Pathological Narcissism.* New York: Aronson.

_____ (1980), *Internal World and External Reality.* New York: Aronson.

Klein, M. (1961), *Narrative of a Child Analysis.* London: Hogarth Press.

Knight, R. P. (1953), Borderline states in psychoanalytic psychiatry and psychology. *Bull. Menn. Clin.,* 17:1–12.

Kohut, H. (1971), *The Analysis of the Self.* New York: International Universities Press.

_____ (1977), *The Restoration of the Self.* New York: International Universities Press.

_____ (1984), *How Does Analysis Cure?* ed. A. Goldberg & P. Stepansky. Chicago: University of Chicago Press.

Kovar, L. (1966), A reconsideration of paranoia. *Psychiatry,* 29:289–305.

Krupp, G. & Krupp, S. L. (1980), Review of *Beyond Grief: Studies in Crisis Intervention,* by E. Lindemann & E. Lindemann. *J. Amer. Acad. Psychoanal.,* 8:633–635.

Levenson, E. (1972), *The Fallacy of Understanding.* New York: Basic Books.

_____ (1982), Follow the fox: An inquiry into the vicissitudes of psychoanalytic supervision. *Contemp. Psychoanal.,* 18:1–15.

_____ (1983), *The Ambiguity of Change.* New York: Basic Books.

_____ (1991), *The Purloined Self: Interpersonal Perspectives in Psychoanalysis.* New York: Contemporary Psychoanalysis Books.

_____ (2003), On seeing what is said: Visual aids to the psychoanalytic process. *Contemp. Psychoanal.,* 39:233–251.

Lionells, M. (1986), A reexamination of hysterical relatedness. *Contemp. Psychoanal.,* 22:570–597.

_____ (1995), Hysteria. In: *Handbook of Interpersonal Psychoanalysis,* ed. M. Lionells, J. Fiscalini, C. H. Mann & D. B. Stern. Hillsdale, NJ: The Analytic Press, pp. 491–515.

_____ Fiscalini, J., Mann, C. H. & Stern, D. B., eds. (1995), *Handbook of Interpersonal Psychoanalysis.* Hillsdale, NJ: The Analytic Press.

Loewald, H. (1960), On the therapeutic action of psychoanalysis. *Internat. J. Psycho-Anal.,* 41:16–33.

Maccoby, M. (1996), The two voices of Erich Fromm: The prophetic and the analytic. In: *A Prophetic Analyst: Erich Fromm's Contributions to Psychoanalysis,* ed. M. Cortina & M. Maccoby. Northvale, NJ: Aronson, pp. 61–93.

Mann, T. (1961), *Little Herr Friedmann and Other Stories.* London: Martin Seiker & Warburg.

Manning, M. (2001), The legacy. In: *Unholy Ghost: Writers on Depression,* ed. N. Casey. New York: HarperCollins, pp. 256–269.

Maroda, K. (1991), *The Power of Countertransference.* New York: Wiley.

_____ (1999), *Seduction, Surrender, and Transformation.* Hillsdale, NJ: The Analytic Press.

_____ (2002), No place to hide: Affectivity, the unconscious, and the development of relational techniques. *Contemp. Psychoanal.,* 38:101–121.

McCaffrey, P. (1984), *Freud and Dora: The Artful Dream.* New Brunswick, NJ: Rutgers University Press.

McCleary, R. W. (1992), *Conversing with Uncertainty.* Hillsdale, NJ: The Analytic Press.

Menninger, K. (1959), Hope. Presented at meeting of the American Psychiatric Association, Philadelphia.

Mitchell, S. A. (1988), *Relational Concepts in Psychoanalysis*. Cambridge, MA: Harvard University Press.

_____ (1993), *Hope and Dread in Psychoanalysis*. New York: Basic Books.

_____ (1997), *Influence and Autonomy in Psychoanalysis*. Hillsdale, NJ: The Analytic Press.

Morris, W., ed. (1969), *The American Heritage Dictionary of the English Language*. Boston: Houghton Mifflin.

Oates, J. C. (1993), Despair: The one unforgivable sin. *New York Times Book Rev.,* p. 3.

O'Leary, J. (1988), Unacknowledged gender effects: Analyst and patient in collusion. *Contemp. Psychoanal.,* 24:668–676.

_____ & Watson, R. I., Jr. (1995), Paranoia. In: *Handbook of Interpersonal Psychoanalysis,* ed. M. Lionells, J. Fiscalini, C. H. Mann & D. B. Stern. Hillsdale, NJ: The Analytic Press, pp. 397–417.

_____ & Wright, F. (1986), Shame and gender issues in pathological narcissism. *Psychoanal. Psychol.,* 3:327–339.

Ortmeyer, D. H. (2002), Clinical relevance of social character and social unconsciousness. *Internat. Forum Psychoanal.,* 2:4–10.

Pearlman, L. A. & Saakvitne, K. (1995), *Trauma and the Therapist: Countertransference and Vicarious Traumatization in Psychotherapy with Incest Survivors*. New York: Norton.

Pizer, S. A. (1998), *Building Bridges: The Negotiation of Paradox in Psychoanalysis*. Hillsdale, NJ: The Analytic Press.

Poland, W. (1984), On the analyst's neutrality. *J. Amer. Psychoanal. Assn.,* 32:283–299.

Racker, H. (1968), *Transference and Countertransference*. New York: International Universities Press.

Rattigan, T. (1985), *In Praise of Love*. In: *Terence Rattigan Plays: Two*. London: Methuen Drama, pp. 171–257.

Reich, A. (1951), On countertransference. *Internat. J. Psycho-Anal.,* 32:25–31.

_____ (1960), Further remarks on countertransference. *Internat. J. Psycho-Anal.,* 41:389–395.

_____ (1966), Empathy and countertransference. In: *Reich: Psychoanalytic Contributions*. New York: International Universities Press, 1973, pp. 344–360.

Renik, O. (1993), Analytic interaction: Conceptualizing technique in light of the analyst's irreducible subjectivity. *Psychoanal. Quart.,* 62:553–571.

_____ (1995), The ideal of the anonymous analyst and the problem of self-disclosure. *Psychoanal. Quart.,* 64:466–495.

_____ (1998), Getting real in analysis. *Psychoanal. Quart.,* 67:566–593.

Rilke, R. M. (1934), *Letters to a Young Poet*. New York: Norton.

Ringstrom, P. A. (2001), Cultivating the improvisational in psychoanalytic treatment. *Psychoanal. Dial.,* 11:727–755.

Roazen, P. (1996), Erich Fromm's courage. In: *A Prophetic Analyst,* ed. M. Cortina & M. Maccoby. Northvale, NJ: Aronson, pp. 427–453.

Rogers, C. (1961), *On Becoming a Person.* Boston: Houghton Mifflin.

Sandler, J. (1976), Countertransference and role-responsiveness. *Internat. Rev. Psycho-Anal.,* 3:43–47.

———— (1983), Reflections on some relations between psychoanalytic concepts and psychoanalytic practice. *Internat. J. Psycho-Anal.,* 4:35–46.

Schachtel, E. G. (1959), *Metamorphosis: On the Conflict of Human Development and the Psychology of Creativity.* Hillsdale, NJ: The Analytic Press, 2001.

Schafer, R. (1983), *The Analytic Attitude.* New York: Basic Books.

Schecter, D. E. (1979), The loving and persecuting superego. *Contemp. Psychoanal.,* 15:361–379.

Searles, H. F. (1986), The countertransference with the borderline patient. In: *Essential Papers on Borderline Disorders,* ed. M. H. Stone. New York: New York University Press, pp. 498–527.

Shabad, P. (2001), *Despair and the Return of Hope.* Northvale, NJ: Aronson.

Shakespeare, W. (1633), *King Lear.* In: *The Arden Edition of the Works of William Shakespeare.* London: Methuen, 1972.

Shaw, D. (2003), On the therapeutic action of analytic love. *Contemp. Psychoanal.,* 39:251–279.

Sherby, L. B. (1989), Love and hate in the treatment of borderline patients. *Contemp. Psychoanal.,* 25:574–591.

Showalter, E. (1993), Hysteria, feminism, and gender. In: *Hysteria Beyond Freud,* ed. S. L. Gilman, H. King, R. Porter, G. S. Rousseau & E. Showalter. Berkeley: University of California Press, pp. 286–345.

Slochower, H. (1970), *Mythopoesis.* Detroit, MI: Wayne State University Press.

Spence (1982), *Narrative Truth and Historical Truth.* New York: Norton.

Spiegel, R. (1960), Communication in the psychoanalysis of depressions. In: *Psychoanalysis and Human Values,* ed. J. H. Masserman. New York: Grune & Stratton, pp. 209–222.

———— (1965), Communication with depressive patients. Panel discussion: The management of depression in children and adults. *Contemp. Psychoanal.,* 2:27–61.

———— (1967), Anger and acting out: Masks of depression. *J. Amer. Acad. Psychoanal.,* 21:597–606.

———— (1968), Supervisory collaboration in the treatment strategy for masked depression. *Contemp. Psychoanal.,* 5:57–61.

———— (1980), Cognitive aspects of affects and other feeling states with clinical applications. *J. Amer. Acad. Psychoanal.,* 8:591–614.

Stern, D. (1998), The process of therapeutic change involving implicit knowledge: Some implications of developmental observations for adult psychotherapy. *Infant Ment. Health J.,* 19:300–308.

_____ Sander, L., Nahum, J., Harrison, A., Bruschweiler-Stern, N. & Tronick, E. (1998), Non-interpretive mechanisms in psychoanalytic therapy. *Internat. J. Psycho-Anal.*, 79:903–921.

Stern, D. B. (1983), Unformulated experience. *Contemp. Psychoanal.*, 19:71–79.

_____ (1989a), The analyst's unformulated experience of the patient. *Contemp. Psychoanal.*, 25:1–33.

_____ (1989b), Discussion of G. Friedman, "Keeping the analysis alive and creative." *Contemp. Psychoanal.*, 25:346–355.

_____ (1990), Courting surprise. *Contemp. Psychoanal.*, 26:425–478.

_____ (1997), *Unformulated Experience: From Dissociation to Imagination in Psychoanalysis.* Hillsdale, NJ: The Analytic Press.

_____ (2002), Language and the nonverbal as a unity: Discussion of "Where is the action in the 'talking cure'?" *Contemp. Psychoanal.*, 38:515–527.

Stone, M. H. (1986), *Essential Papers on Borderline Disorders: One Hundred Years at the Border.* New York: New York University Press.

Styron, W. (2001), From darkness visible. In: *Unholy Ghost: Writers on Depression,* ed. N. Casey. New York: HarperCollins.

Sullivan, H. S. (1940), *Conceptions of Modern Psychiatry,* New York: Norton.

_____ (1953), *The Interpersonal Theory of Psychiatry.* New York: Norton.

_____ (1954), *The Psychiatric Interview.* New York: Norton.

_____ (1956), *Clinical Studies in Psychiatry.* . New York: Norton.

Szalita, A. (1976), Some thoughts on empathy. *Psychiatry,* 39:142–152.

Tennyson, A. (1942), "Tears, idle tears." In: *A Great Treasury of Poems, Volume Two,* ed. L. Untermeyer. New York: Simon & Schuster.

Tomkins, S. S. (1962), *Affect, Imagery, Consciousness, Vol. 1: The Positive Affects.* New York: Springer.

_____ (1963), *Affect, Imagery, Consciousness, Vol. 2: The Negative Affects.* New York: Springer.

van der Kolk, B. (1995), The body, memory, and the psychobiology of trauma. In: *Sexual Abuse Recalled,* ed. J. Alpert. Northvale, NJ: Aronson, pp. 29–60.

Wachtel, P. L. (1993), *Therapeutic Communication.* New York: Guilford Press.

Wilbur, R. (1989), The writer. In: *A Safe Place,* ed. L. Havens. New York: Random House.

Winnicott, D. (1949), Hate in the countertransference. *Internat. J. Psycho-Anal.,* 30:69–75.

_____ (1960), Ego distortion in terms of true and false self. In: *The Maturational Processes and the Facilitating Environment.* Madison, CT: International Universities Press, pp. 149–152, 1965.

_____ (1965), *The Maturational Processes and the Facilitating Environment.* Madison, CT: International Universities Press.

_____ (1971), *Playing and Reality.* London: Tavistock.

Witenberg, E., ed. (1973), *Interpersonal Explorations in Psychoanalysis*. New York: Basic Books.

Wolstein, B. (1975), Countertransference: The psychoanalyst's shared experience and inquiry with the patient. *J. Amer. Acad. Psychoanal.*, 3:77–90.

———— (1987), Experience, interpretation, and self-knowledge. *Contemp. Psychoanal.*, 23:329–349.

———— (1988), *Essential Papers on Countertransference*. New York: New York University Press.

Youngerman, J. (1995), Borderline conditions. In: *Handbook of Interpersonal Psychoanalysis*, ed. M. Lionells, J. Fiscalini, C. H. Mann & D. B. Stern. Hillsdale, NJ: The Analytic Press, pp. 419–435.

Zeddies, T. J. (2002), Sluggers and analysts: Batting for average with the psychoanalytic unconscious. *Contemp. Psychoanal.*, 38:465–477.

Index

About the Author

Sandra Buechler, Ph.D. is a training and supervising analyst at the William Alanson White Institute in New York City. She supervises at Columbia Presbyterian Medical Center and at the Institute of Contemporary Psychotherapy. A member of the editorial board of *Contemporary Psychoanalysis,* Dr. Buechler has written numerous articles on feeling states in psychoanalysis, including papers on hope, loneliness, joy, and mourning in both treatment participants.